Best of
McCall's QUILTING

Simple Beginner Quilts

Fantastic quilts can be easy to make! These 16 exclusive designs from the pages of *McCall's Quilting* use basic piecing skills to make wonderful wall hangings, cozy cuddle quilts, and beautiful bed coverings. New and experienced quilters alike will love these simply spectacular projects.

LEISURE ARTS
the art of everyday living
www.leisurearts.com

Best of McCall's QUILTING

SIMPLE BEGINNER QUILTS

EDITORIAL

Editor-in-Chief	**Beth Hayes**
Art Director	**Ellie Brown**
Senior Editor	**Kathryn Patterson**
Associate Editor	**Sherri Bain Driver**
Assistant Editor	**Erin Russek**
Web Editor	**Valerie Uland**
Administrative Editor	**Susan Zinanti**
Graphic Designers	**Karen Gillis Taylor**
	Tracee Doran
	Joyce Robinson
Photography Stylist	**Ashley Slupe**
Photographer	**Mellisa Karlin Mahoney**

CREATIVE CRAFTS GROUP, LLC

President & CEO	**Stephen J. Kent**
CFO	**Mark F. Arnett**
SVP, General Manager	**Tina Battock**
VP, Publishing Director	**Joel P. Toner**
SVP, Chief Marketing Officer	**Nicole McGuire**
VP, Production	**Barbara Schmitz**
Corporate Controller	**Jordan Bohrer**
Product & Video Development	**Kristi Loeffelholz**

OPERATIONS

Circulation Director	**Deb Westmaas**
New Business Mgr.	**Lance Covert**
Renewal & Billing Mgr.	**Nekeya Dancy**
Newsstand Consultant	**T. J. Montilli**
Digital Marketing Mgr.	**Laurie Harris**
Online Subscription Mgr.	**Jodi Lee**
Director of IT	**Tom Judd**
Production Manager	**Dominic Taormina**
Ad Prod. Coordinator	**Sarah Katz**
Advertising Coordinator	**Madalene Becker**
Administrative Assistant	**Jane Flynn**
Retail Sales	**LaRita Godfrey,** **800-815-3538**

ADVERTISING

Publisher	**Lisa O'Bryan,** **303-215-5641**
Advertising	**Cristy Adamski,** **715-824-4546**
Online Advertising	**Andrea Abrahamson,** **303-215-5686**

EDITORIAL OFFICES

McCall's Quilting
741 Corporate Circle, Suite A, Golden, CO 80401
(303) 215-5600 (303) 215-5601 fax

Produced by the editors of
McCall's Quilting magazine
for
Leisure Arts, Inc.
5701 Ranch Drive, Little Rock, AR 72223-9633
www.leisurearts.com.
Library of Congress Control Number: 2013937084
ISBN-13/EAN: 978-1-4647-0861-9

Contents

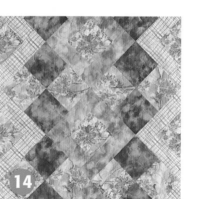

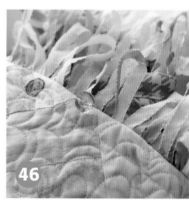

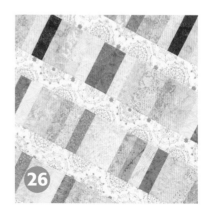

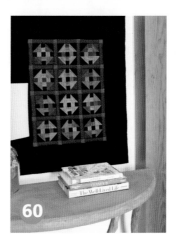

Designed by
COREY YODER

Machine Quilted by
ANGELA WALTERS

Triangle Toss

Add a bright, colorful note to any room with this cool modern throw. Our step-by-step photos show how to use simple template shapes to machine-piece the triangle units.

Finished Quilt Size
54½" x 63½"

Note: See **page 7** for piecing templates.

Number of Blocks and Finished Size
42 Triangle Blocks 9" x 9"

*Fabric Requirements	
White (background)	2⅜ yds.
Dark purple (blocks, binding)	1 yd.
Turquoise, purple, gold, dark pink, pink, orange, lime, **and** aqua (blocks)	⅜ yd. **each**
Backing (piece widthwise)	3⅝ yds.
Batting size	64" x 72"
Template plastic	
*All fabrics are solids.	

Planning, Cutting, and Marking

Corey chose solid fabrics in scrumptious colors for her fun, modern quilt. Check out our photo lesson, **Using Templates** (page 6), for help making the blocks.

To prepare piecing templates, trace A/Ar and B on template plastic, including seam lines, grain-line arrows, and match points. Cut out on outer marked lines, and use large needle or stiletto to make small holes in plastic at match points. Place templates right side down on wrong side of appropriate fabrics; mark around edges. Cut out patches on marked lines. Mark match points on wrong side of all template patches.

Cutting Instructions
(cut in order listed)

White
    42 strips 2¾" x 9½"
    42 **each** Templates A **and** A reversed (Ar)

Dark purple
    7 strips 2½" x width of fabric (binding)
    5 Template B

Turquoise, purple, dark pink, orange, **and** aqua—cut from each:
    5 Template B

Gold, pink, **and** lime—cut from each:
    4 Template B

Piecing the Blocks

1 See **Using Templates** for help with this step. Sew white A and Ar triangles to B triangle (**Diagram I**), and then sew white 9½" strip to remaining side of B to complete Triangle Block. Make 42 total.

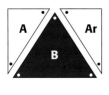

2¾" x 9½"

Make 42 total

Diagram I

Assembling the Quilt Top

2 Refer to the **Assembly Diagram**, watching placement and orientation. Sew 7 rows of 6 blocks each. Stitch rows together.

Quilting and Finishing

3 Layer, baste, and quilt. Angela machine quilted 2 alternating geometric designs in colored triangles. The background features spirals. Bind with dark purple.

Assembly Diagram

Using Templates

Photo A Make Templates A/Ar and B as described in **Planning, Cutting, and Marking**.

Photo C Position white A on colored triangle B, right sides together and aligning match points and raw edges. Pin patches together at match points.

Photo E Open and press seam allowances toward darker fabric. In same manner, pin Ar to B.

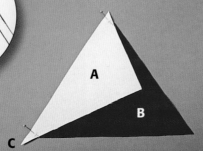

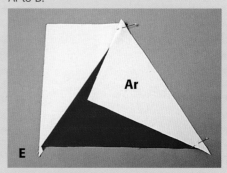

Photo B Cut out patches listed and mark match points.

Photo D Stitch ¼" from raw edges.

Photo F Sew seam. Open and press. Complete block as described in **Step 1**.

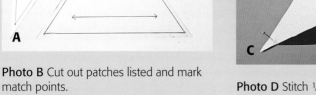

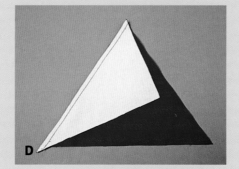

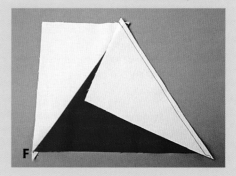

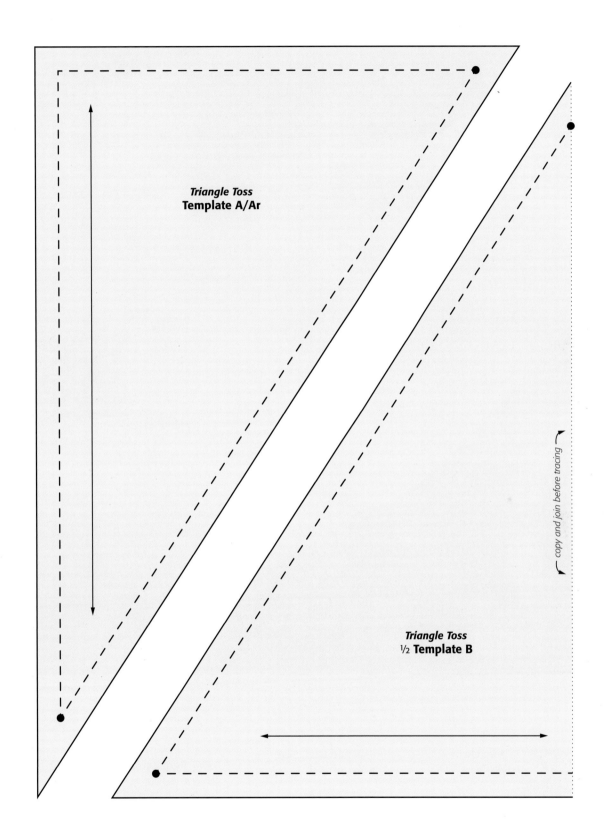

Triangle Toss
Template A/Ar

Triangle Toss
½ **Template B**

copy and join before tracing

Photographed at Scandinavian Designs, 9000 E. Hampden, Denver, CO 80231; www.ScandinavianDesigns.com.

Designed by
KAREN DUMONT

Machine Quilted by
SARA PARRISH

Finished Quilt Size
80¼" x 97⅝"

**Number of Blocks
and Finished Size**
32 Framed Square
Blocks
   12¼" x 12¼"

Fabric Requirements*
16 assorted florals/stripes (blocks)   ½ yd. **each**
Cream/pink stripe (setting triangles)   1⅝ yds.
Black/orange floral (border, binding)   2⅝ yds.
Backing (piece widthwise)   7½ yds.
Batting size   90" x 106"
*Based on 40" of usable width. See **Planning
and Cutting**.

On Cloud Nine

Drift off to peaceful summer slumbers

under this featherweight quilt made of cotton lawn. You've got to feel it to believe it!

Planning and Cutting

Karen made her pretty quilt using beautiful prints and stripes made of 52"-wide cotton lawn. Lawn is a lightweight and somewhat sheer fabric, just perfect for a summer quilt. Our pattern is written for a standard fabric width of 40-42", but you'll find fabric requirements and cutting instructions for the 52"-wide fabrics, as well as tips on handling a lightweight fabric such as lawn, on our website, **McCallsQuilting.com** (see page 10).

If you wish to use the cream/pink stripe and/or black/orange floral to piece some of your blocks, as Karen did, purchase ½ yd. extra of each, as part of your assorted florals/stripes.

Cutting Instructions
(cut in order listed)

⊠ = cut in half twice diagonally
◺ = cut in half diagonally
16 assorted florals/stripes—**cut from each:**
  2 squares 9¾" x 9¾"
  8 strips 2" x 9¾"
  8 squares 2" x 2"
Cream/pink stripe
  4 squares 20" x 20" ⊠
  *2 squares 11" x 11" ◺
Black/orange floral
  **4 strips 5¾" x 92", pieced from
    10 width of fabric (WOF) strips
  10 strips 2½" x WOF (binding)
*See **Cutting Diagram**, below.
**Border strips include extra length for trimming.

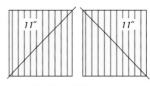

Cutting Diagram

Assembly Diagram

Piecing the Blocks

1. Sew 3 rows using 4 matching floral or stripe 2″ squares, 4 matching 9¾″ strips of a second floral/stripe, and one 9¾″ square of a third floral/stripe (**Diagram I**). Stitch rows together to make Framed Square Block. Make 32 total.

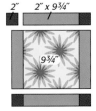

Make 32 total

Diagram I

Assembling the Quilt Top

Note: Refer to **Assembly Diagram** for following steps. The setting triangles on all edges and corners are cut oversized for subsequent trimming.

2. Watching orientation of stripes in triangles, arrange and sew 8 diagonal rows using cream/pink stripe 20″ quarter-square triangles and blocks. You will have 2 quarter-square triangles left over. Sew rows together. Stitch stripe 11″ half-square triangles to corners. **Trim** edges even.

3. Sew black/orange floral 92″ strips to sides; trim even with top and bottom. Stitch remaining 92″ strips to top/bottom; trim even with sides.

Quilting and Finishing

4. Layer, baste, and quilt. Sara machine quilted an allover floral design. Bind with black/orange floral.

Visit

McCallsQuilting.com...for fabric requirements and cutting instructions for 52″-wide fabric, as well as tips on handling a lightweight fabric such as lawn. Click on Bonuses, McCall's Bonuses, and On Cloud Nine.

Also visit for information about diagonal sets. Just click on Lessons and Setting Blocks "On-Point."

Designed by
CINDY LAMMON

Finished Quilt Size
37½" x 45½"

**Number of Blocks
and Finished Size**
12 Double Windmill
Blocks 6" x 6"

Pinwheel Princess

**In her kingdom, pinwheels can be treasures, and pink the color
of royalty.** Inspire her dreams with your own version of this princess-pleasing quilt.

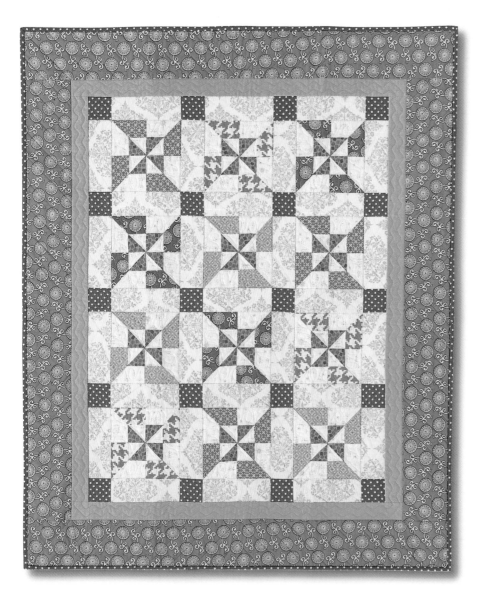

Cutting Instructions

◪ = cut in half diagonally

White print
  *48 rectangles 2″ x 3⅞″
  24 squares 2⅜″ x 2⅜″ ◪
Pink print
  24 squares 2⅜″ x 2⅜″ ◪
4 assorted aqua prints—cut from each:
  *12 rectangles 2″ x 3⅞″
Pink dot
  **5 strips 2½″ x width of fabric (WOF)
    for binding
  20 squares 2½″ x 2½″
Yellow print
  31 strips 2½″ x 6½″
Aqua solid
  4 strips 2″ x 38″
Aqua/pink print
  4 strips 4½″ x WOF
*See **Cutting Diagram,** below left.
**Cut first.

Piecing the Blocks

1 Referring to **Diagram I-A,** sew together 1 trimmed white print 2″ x 3⅞″ rectangle and 1 pink print 2⅜″ half-square triangle to make pieced triangle. Make 48.
In similar manner make turquoise/white pieced triangle (**Diagram I-B**). Make 4 matching for each block.

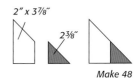

Make 48

Diagram I-A

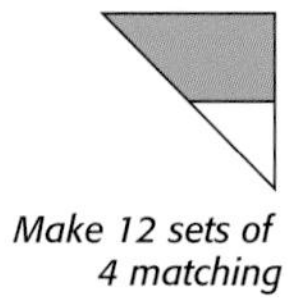

Make 12 sets of
4 matching

Diagram I-B

Fabric Requirements

White print (blocks)	⅝ yd.
Pink print (blocks)	1 fat quarter*
4 assorted aqua prints (blocks)	1 fat eighth** each
Pink dot (sashing posts, binding)	¾ yd.
Yellow print (sashing)	⅝ yd.
Aqua solid (inner border)	⅜ yd.
Aqua/pink print (outer border)	⅝ yd.
Backing (piece widthwise)	2⅝ yds.
Batting size	Crib

*A fat quarter is an 18″ x 20-22″ cut of fabric.
**A fat eighth is a 9″ x 20-22″ cut of fabric.

Planning and Cutting

Cindy used fabric from her stash to make this cheerful baby quilt. If you want to use the outer border print for some blocks, as Cindy did, purchase an additional fat eighth of this fabric to use in block piecing.

To prepare 2″ x 3⅞″ rectangles for piecing, place all rectangles right side up and trim as shown in the **Cutting Diagram.**

trim all white
rectangles with
fabric right
side up

trim all aqua
rectangles with
fabric right
side up

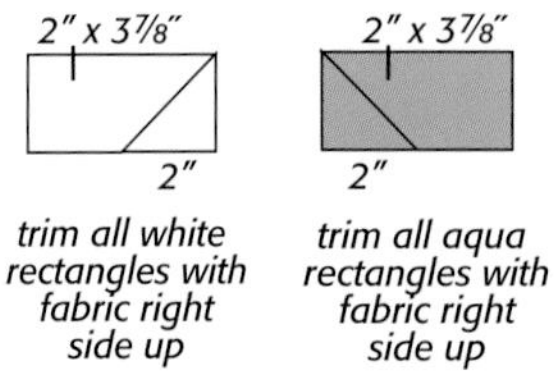

Cutting Diagram

2 Stitch together 4 white/pink and 4 matching turquoise/white pieced triangles to make Double Windmill Block (**Diagram II**). Make 12 total.

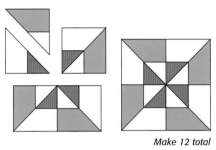

Make 12 total

Diagram II

Quilt Top Assembly

Note: Refer to **Assembly Diagram** for following steps.

3 Sew 5 sashing rows of 4 pink dot 2½" squares and 3 yellow 2½" x 6½" strips each. Stitch 4 block rows of 4 yellow strips and 3 blocks each. Sew rows together.

4 Stitch aqua solid 38" strips to sides; trim even with top and bottom. Add remaining aqua solid strips to top/bottom; trim even with sides. Sew aqua/pink print WOF strips to sides; trim even. Stitch remaining aqua/pink strips to top/bottom; trim even.

Quilting and Finishing

5 Layer, baste, and quilt. Cindy machine quilted each block with curved lines in the center white patches and loops in the outer patches. The sashing is quilted in a diamond design and a spiral is centered on each sashing post. Two serpentine lines are stitched in the inner border, and the outer border features diagonal lines. Bind with pink dot.

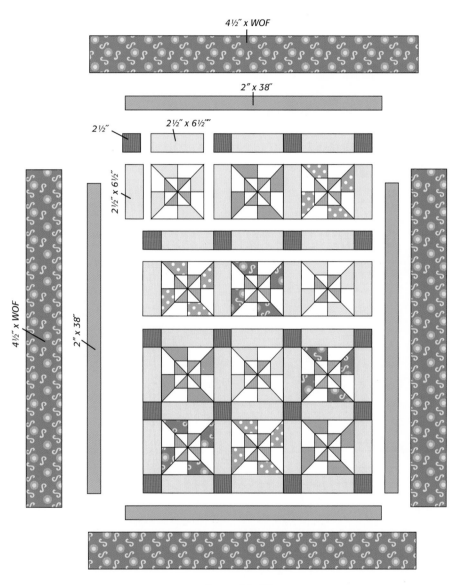

Assembly Diagram

Visit

McCallsQuilting.com...
For more kid-friendly patterns, visit our website, **McCallsQuilting.com,** click on Blocks & Patterns, then Quilt Pattern Index and check out the Kids Corner.

Peonies & Plaids

Just four fantastic fabrics are all you'll need to make your own version of this ladylike bed quilt. Fewer fabrics means less time spent cutting and keeping things organized. You'll be having sweet dreams under this one in no time.

Designed by
SUSAN GUZMAN

Machine Quilted by
LINDA BARRETT

Finished Quilt Size
88⅜" x 88⅜"

**Number of Blocks
and Finished Size**
16 Four-Patch Blocks
    12" x 12"
9 Framed Square Blocks
    12" x 12"

Fabric Requirements

Green/pink large floral (blocks, middle border)	4⅛ yds.
Light green mottle (blocks)	1⅛ yds.
Dark green mottle (Four-Patch Blocks, inner and outer borders, binding)	2⅜ yds.
Pink plaid (Framed Square Blocks, setting triangles)	3⅛ yds.*
Backing	8¼ yds.
Batting size	98″ x 98″

*See **Planning and Cutting**.

Planning and Cutting

Susan chose bright, pretty fabrics for this easy-to-piece bed quilt. The pink plaid squares (for the setting triangles) are cut on the bias grain to keep the plaid running in the same direction throughout the quilt. Watch plaid direction carefully during cutting and assembly.

Cutting Instructions
(cut in order listed)

⊠ = cut in half twice diagonally
◻ = cut in half diagonally
Green/pink large floral
 8 strips 6½″ x width of fabric (WOF)
 *2 strips 8½″ x 92″, cut on lengthwise
  grain
 *2 strips 8½″ x 76″, cut on lengthwise
  grain
Light green mottle
 3 strips 6½″ x WOF
 2 strips 3½″ x WOF
 6 strips 3½″ x 12½″
Dark green mottle
 3 strips 6½″ x WOF
 10 strips 2½″ x WOF (binding)
 *4 strips 1½″ x 94″, pieced from 10
  WOF strips
 *4 strips 1½″ x 76″, pieced from 8
  WOF strips
Pink plaid
 2 strips 3½″ x WOF
 12 strips 3½″ x 12½″
 **3 squares 20″ x 20″ ⊠
 **2 squares 10″ x 10″ ◻
*Border strips include extra length for trimming.
Cut squares on the bias grain; see **Planning and Cutting.

Piecing the Blocks

1 Referring to **Diagram I**, sew green/pink large floral and light green mottle 6½″ x WOF strips together. Make 3. Press in direction of arrow. Cut into 16 segments 6½″ wide. In similar manner, make remaining strip sets and cut segments in arrangements and quantities shown.

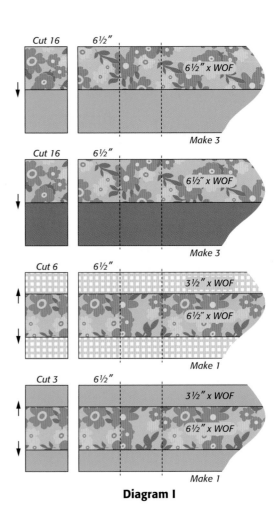

Diagram I

2 Sew 2 floral/light green segments together to make Four-Patch Block (**Diagram II**). Make 8. In same manner, make 8 floral/dark green Four-Patch Blocks.

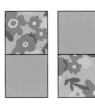 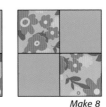 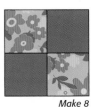

Make 8   Make 8

Diagram II

1½" x 94"

8½" x 92"

10"

1½" x 76"

20"

1½" x 94"

8½" x 76"

1½" x 76"

Assembly Diagram

3 Stitch pink plaid 12½" strips to plaid/floral segment to make Framed Square Block (**Diagram III**). Make 6. Make 3 Framed Square Blocks using light green 12½" strips and light green/floral segments.

Assembling the Quilt Top

Note: Refer to **Assembly Diagram** for following steps. The setting triangles on all edges and corners are cut oversized for subsequent trimming.

4 Sew 7 diagonal rows using plaid 20" quarter-square triangles and blocks. Sew rows together. Stitch plaid 10" half-square triangles to corners. **Trim** edges even.

3½" x 12½"

Make 6

Make 3

Diagram III

5 Sew dark green 76" strips to sides; trim even with top and bottom. Sew remaining dark green 76" strips to top/bottom; trim even with sides. In same manner, sew remaining borders to quilt, adding side strips first for each border and trimming even after each addition.

Quilting and Finishing

6 Layer, baste, and quilt. Linda machine quilted an overall feathered plume pattern. Bind with dark green mottle.

Mint Chocolate Chip

It's cool, sweet, and oh so yummy! This graphic design showcases large prints beautifully, and the solid borders are perfect for highlighting a bit of hand quilting.

Designed by
VALERIE ULAND

Finished Quilt Size
55½" x 66½"

**Number of Blocks
and Finished Size**
20 Pieced Blocks
10" x 10"

Fabric Requirements

Green large print (block, binding)	⁷⁄₈ yd.
Gray solid (blocks, sashing)	1³⁄₈ yds.
Dark brown solid (blocks, sashing posts, inner border)	⁵⁄₈ yd.
Assorted florals and prints (blocks)	1⁵⁄₈-1⁷⁄₈ yds. **total**
Green solid (outer border)	1 yd.
Backing (piece widthwise)	3³⁄₄ yds.
Batting size	64" x 76"

Planning and Cutting

Valerie cut her matching sets of 5" squares from an assortment of Layer Cake 10" precut squares she had collected over time. Do likewise if you wish, or cut sets of 5" squares from other fabric pieces in your stash. One of Valerie's blocks was made with the same fabric she used for her binding; our instructions have you do the same to help tie the colors and patterns in your quilt together.

Cutting Instructions

(cut in order listed)

Green large print
    7 strips 2½" x width of fabric (WOF)
        for binding
    4 squares 5" x 5"
Gray solid
    49 strips 1½" x 10½"
    80 strips 1½" x 5"
Dark brown solid
    *4 strips 2½" x 60", pieced from 6
        WOF strips
    50 squares 1½" x 1½"
Assorted florals and prints—**cut 19 sets of:**
    4 matching squares 5" x 5"
Green solid
    *4 strips 3½" x 64", pieced from 8
        WOF strips
*Border strips include extra length for trimming.

Piecing the Blocks

1 Referring to **Diagram I**, sew 3 rows using 4 matching 5" squares, 4 gray 5" strips, and 1 dark brown 1½" square. Sew rows together to make Pieced Block. Make 20 total.

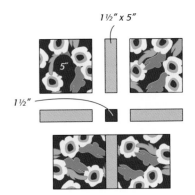

Make 20 total

Diagram I

Assembling the Quilt Top

Note: Refer to **Assembly Diagram** for following steps.

2 Stitch 6 sashing rows using 5 dark brown 1½" squares and 4 gray 10½" strips each. Stitch 5 block rows using 5 gray 10½" strips and 4 blocks each. Sew rows together, alternating.

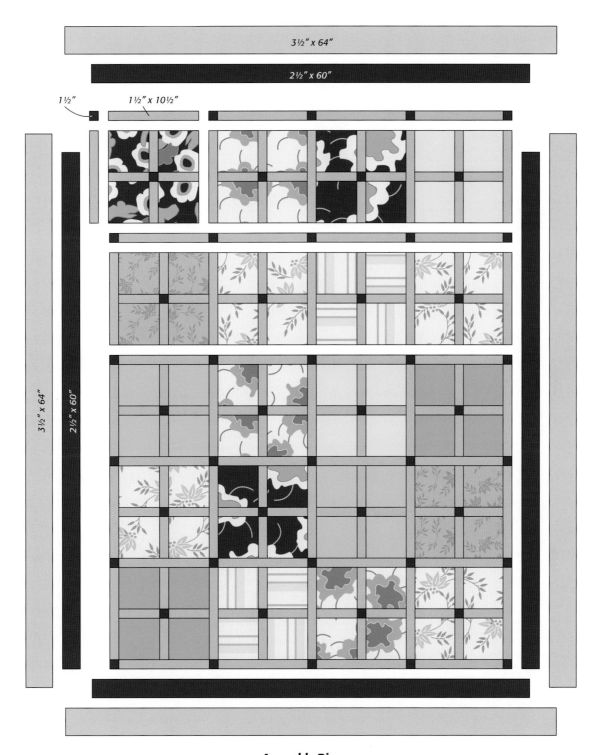

Assembly Diagram

3 Sew dark brown 60″ strips to sides; trim even with top and bottom. Sew remaining dark brown strips to top/bottom; trim even with sides. Sew green 64″ strips to sides; trim even. Sew remaining green strips to top/bottom; trim even.

Quilting and Finishing

4 Layer, baste, and quilt. Valerie machine quilted ¼″ from seams in the quilt center. She used #8 perle cotton to hand quilt the borders in a long running stitch. Bind with green large print.

Café au Lait

Finished Quilt Size
96" x 96"

Number of Blocks and Finished Size
16 Café au Lait Blocks 18" x 18"

Fabric Requirements
Assorted cream prints (blocks)	1¼-1⅝ yds. **total**
Brown texture (blocks, sashing)	5⅛ yds.
Assorted light blue prints (blocks, sashing)	1⅛-1⅜ yds. **total**
Red texture (blocks, sashing posts, binding)	1⅝ yds.
Cream/red border stripe (border)	6⅛ yds.*
Backing	8⅞ yds.
Batting size	104" x 104"

*Fabric must have 4 stripes running lengthwise, each at least 9¼" wide.

Steaming fresh coffee, a pitcher of cream, and a few perfect strawberries… breakfast in bed is a genuine treat and this lovely quilt is the perfect accessory.

Designed by
GERRI ROBINSON

Machine Quilted by
REBECCA SEGURA of
Zeffie's Quilts

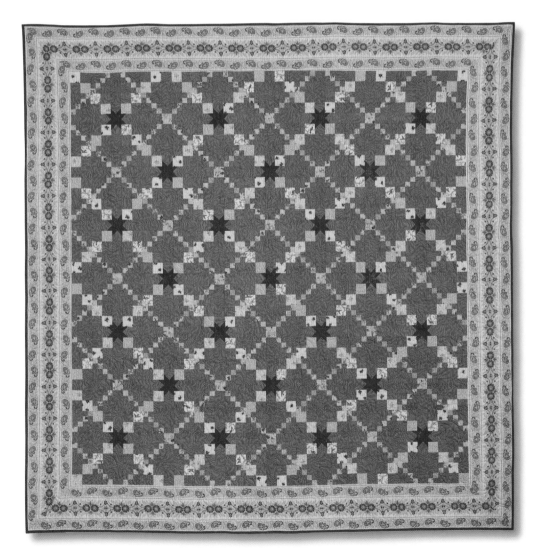

A Quiet Constellation
Gerri used a beautiful cream/red border stripe and coordinating fabrics to create this lovely, peaceful bed quilt. The Irish chain and the red star accents are created in the blocks and continue into the sashing and sashing posts.

Cutting Instructions
(cut in order listed)
Assorted cream prints—**cut a total of:**
    16 strips 2½" x width of fabric
    (WOF)
Brown texture
    16 strips 2½" x WOF
    20 strips 1½" x WOF
    112 strips 2½" x 8½"
    256 squares 2½" x 2½"
Assorted light blue prints—**cut a total of:**
    24 strips 1½" x WOF
Red texture
    11 strips 2½" x WOF (binding)
    25 squares 2½" x 2½"
    200 squares 1½" x 1½"
Cream/red border stripe
    *4 strips 9¼" x 108", cut on
    lengthwise grain, centered on stripe
*Border strips include extra length for trimming.

Piecing the Blocks and Sashing

1 Referring to **Diagram I-A**, sew together 1 each assorted cream print and brown texture 2½" x WOF strips to make strip set. Make 16 total. Press in direction of arrow. Cut into 256 segments 2½" wide.

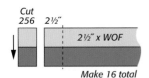

Diagram I-A

In similar manner, make remaining strip sets and cut segments in fabric combinations, sizes, and quantities shown in **Diagram I-B**.

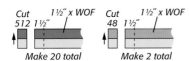

Diagram I-B

2 Sew 2 cream/brown segments together to make large 4-patch (**Diagram II-A**). Make 128 total.

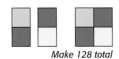

Make 128 total

Diagram II-A

In same manner, make remaining 4-patches in fabric combinations and quantities shown in **Diagram II-B**.

Make 256 total   *Make 24 total*

Diagram II-B

3 Referring to **Diagram III**, stitch together 2 each brown 2½" squares and brown/blue 4-patches to make pieced square. Make 128 total.

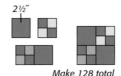

Make 128 total

Diagram III

Join 2 each large 4-patches and pieced squares to make quarter-block (**Diagram IV**). Make 64 total.

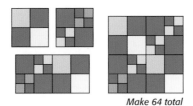

Make 64 total

Diagram IV

4 Draw diagonal line on wrong side of red texture 1½" square. Referring to **Diagram V**, place marked square on brown 2½" x 8½" strip, right sides together, aligning raw edges. Stitch on drawn line; trim away and discard excess fabric. Open and press. In same manner, add red 1½" square to adjacent corner to make pieced strip. Make 100.

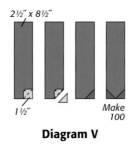

Diagram V

5 Referring to **Diagram VI** and watching orientation, sew together 4 quarter-blocks, 4 pieced strips, and 1 red 2½" square to make Café au Lait Block. Make 16 total.

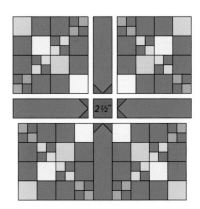

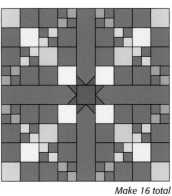

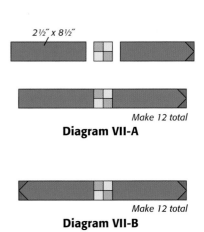

Make 16 total

Diagram VI

6 To make edge sashing strip, sew together 1 brown 2½" x 8½" strip, 1 blue/blue 4-patch and 1 pieced strip, watching orientation of pieced strip (**Diagram VII-A**). Make 12 total. In similar manner, make 12 total center sashing strips (**Diagram VII-B**).

Make 12 total

Diagram VII-A

Make 12 total

Diagram VII-B

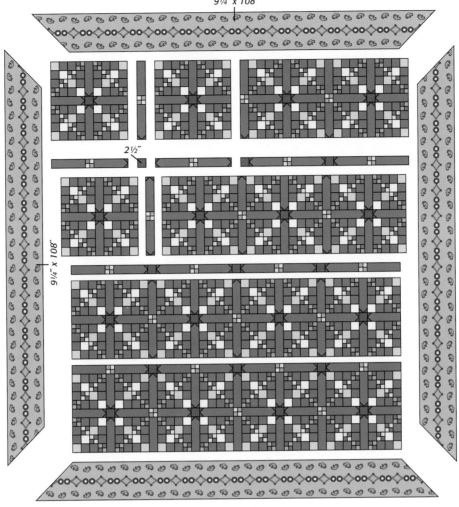

9¼" x 108"

2½"

9¼" x 108"

Assembly Diagram

Assembling the Quilt Top
Note: Refer to **Assembly Diagram** for following steps.

7 Sew 2 top/bottom block rows using 4 blocks and 3 edge sashing strips each.

Stitch 3 sashing rows using 2 each edge and center sashing strips and 3 red 2½" squares each. Sew 2 center rows using 4 blocks and 3 center sashing strips each. Stitch rows together, in order shown.

8 Centering as desired, add border strips to all sides of quilt (see **Add Mitered Border**, below). Sew and trim miters.

Quilting and Finishing
9 Layer, baste, and quilt. Rebecca machine quilted an allover feather design. Bind with red texture.

Add Mitered Border
Center and pin border strips to sides, top, and bottom of quilt. Strips will extend beyond quilt top. Starting and stopping ¼" from quilt corners and backstitching to secure, sew strips to quilt top. Press seam allowances toward quilt top. Fold quilt on diagonal, right sides together. Align border strip raw edges and border seams at the ¼" backstitched point; pin together. Align ruler edge with fold, extending ruler completely across border. Draw line from the backstitched point to the border raw edges. Stitch on drawn line, backstitching at both ends. Press seam open. With quilt right side up, align 45°-angle line of square ruler on seam line to check accuracy. If corner is flat and square, trim excess fabric to ¼" seam allowance. Repeat for all corners.

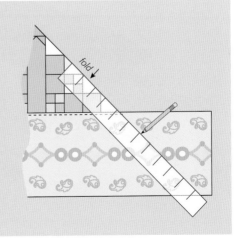

Designed by
LAURA STONE ROBERTS

Machine Quilted by
ALAINA MARLER

Finished Quilt Size
83" x 83½"

**Number of Blocks
and Finished Size**
42 Strip-Pieced Blocks
   7½" x 12"

Fruit-colored batiks and a cool border print give this quilt all the frosty appeal of sorbet on a hot summer day. Strip piecing speeds construction, and an all-machine-stitched binding will get you to the finish line quickly.

Gelato

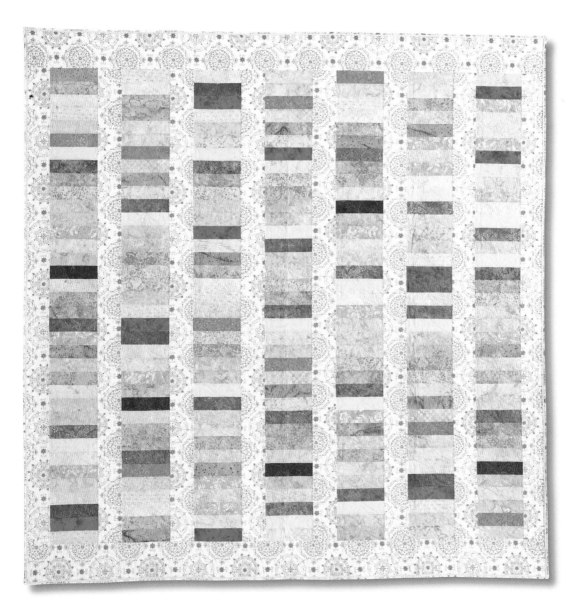

Fabric Requirements

Assorted batiks (blocks)	3⅞-4¼ yds. **total***
White/multicolor print (sashing, border, flanged binding)	3½ yds.
Light blue mottle (flanged binding)	⅝ yd.
Backing	7¾ yds.
Batting size	92″ x 92″

*See **Planning**.

Planning

Laura substituted 54 precut 2½″ x width of fabric strips for the assorted batik yardage. The flanged binding adds an interesting touch and is completely machine stitched, making it a super-fast way to finish a quilt. Give it a try, and you may never hand-stitch the back side of binding down again!

Cutting Instructions
(cut in order listed)

Assorted batiks—cut a total of:
   *54 strips 2½″ x width of fabric (WOF)

White/multicolor print
   10 strips 1¼″ x WOF (flanged binding)
   **2 strips 6″ x 88″, pieced from 5 WOF strips
   **8 strips 4¼″ x 76″, cut on lengthwise grain

Light blue mottle
   10 strips 1¾″ x WOF (flanged binding)

*See **Planning**.
**Strips include extra length for trimming.

Piecing the Blocks and Quilt Top

① Referring to **Diagram I**, sew together 6 assorted batik WOF strips to make strip set. Make 9 total. Press all seams in same direction. Cut into 42 total Strip-Pieced Blocks 8″ wide.

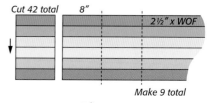

Diagram I

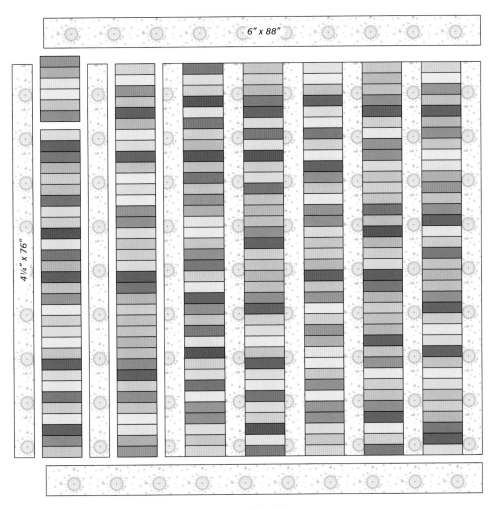

6" x 88"

4¼" x 76"

Assembly Diagram

2 **Note:** Refer to **Assembly Diagram** for following steps. Sew 7 vertical rows of 6 blocks each. Sew 8 white/multicolor print 76" strips and 7 block rows together, alternating and trimming strips even with block rows after each addition.

3 Stitch white print 88" strips to top and bottom; trim even with sides.

Quilting and Finishing

4 Layer, baste, and quilt. Alaina machine quilted a repeating curves and swirls motif on the block rows, and a feathered floral pattern on the white print areas. **Trim** batting and backing even with quilt top.

5 Sew together 10 light blue mottle 1¾" x WOF strips, end to end, to make wide pieced strip. Sew together 10 white print 1¼" x WOF strips, end to end, to make narrow pieced strip. Sew wide and

narrow pieced strips together as shown in **Diagram II**.

1¾"

1¼"

Diagram II

Fold pieced strip in half lengthwise **wrong** sides together, and press to make flanged binding (**Diagram III**).

fold

Diagram III

6 Referring to **Diagram IV**, stitch flanged binding to **wrong** side of quilt, aligning raw edges (place seamed side of binding against quilt). Miter corners and join binding ends as in traditional binding.

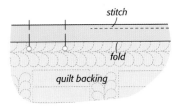

stitch

fold

quilt backing

Diagram IV

Turn flanged binding to quilt front (**Diagram V**). Stitch in the ditch (through all layers) between white print strip and light blue flange, mitering corners, to complete the flanged binding.

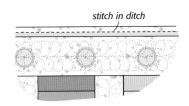

stitch in ditch

Diagram V

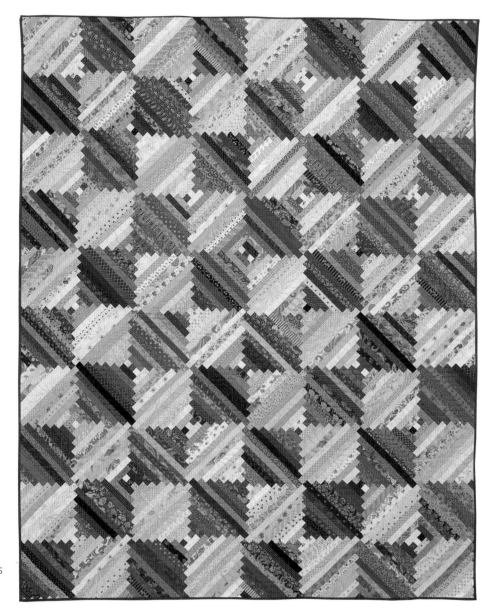

Designed by
LISSA ALEXANDER

Machine Quilted by
MAGGI HONEYMAN

Finished Quilt Size
74" x 92⅜"

**Number of Blocks
and Finished Size**
40 Courthouse Steps
Blocks
   13" x 13"

Carolina Courthouse

The classic Courthouse Steps block evokes wide, impressive

flights of stairs and is a perennial favorite. This lovely example, made with assorted

fabrics, is a fast, easy stash reducer in any color range you choose.

Fabric Requirements	
Assorted dark prints (blocks)	4⅝-5 yds. **total**
Assorted light prints (blocks)	4⅝-5 yds. **total**
Brown texture (binding)	1 yd.
Backing (piece widthwise)	7 yds.
Batting size	82" x 102"

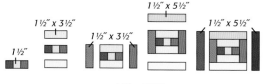

Planning

In this intriguing version of Courthouse Steps, half-blocks and quarter-blocks are used to square the edges of the diagonal set. The resulting design looks like a piecing puzzle, but is really quite simple to sew. Make your quilt with different colors if you wish, but be sure to maintain the light/dark placement of fabric values throughout.

Cutting Instructions

Assorted dark prints **and** assorted light prints—**cut from each value group:**

> 60 squares 1½″ x 1½″
> 80 strips 1½″ x 3½″
> 80 strips 1½″ x 5½″
> 80 strips 1½″ x 7½″
> 80 strips 1½″ x 9½″
> 80 strips 1½″ x 11½″
> 40 strips 1½″ x 13½″

Brown texture

> 10 strips 2½″ x width of fabric (binding)

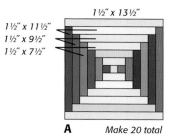

A   *Make 20 total*

Diagram I-A

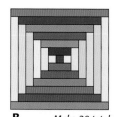

B   *Make 20 total*

Diagram I-B

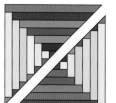

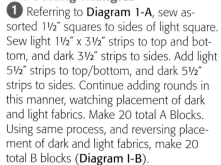

B   *Cut 3*   **B**   *Cut 4*   **B**   *Cut 1*

Diagram II-A   **Diagram II-B**

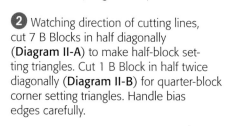

Piecing the Blocks and Setting Triangles

❶ Referring to **Diagram 1-A**, sew assorted 1½″ squares to sides of light square. Sew light 1½″ x 3½″ strips to top and bottom, and dark 3½″ strips to sides. Add light 5½″ strips to top/bottom, and dark 5½″ strips to sides. Continue adding rounds in this manner, watching placement of dark and light fabrics. Make 20 total A Blocks. Using same process, and reversing placement of dark and light fabrics, make 20 total B blocks (**Diagram I-B**).

❷ Watching direction of cutting lines, cut 7 B Blocks in half diagonally (**Diagram II-A**) to make half-block setting triangles. Cut 1 B Block in half twice diagonally (**Diagram II-B**) for quarter-block corner setting triangles. Handle bias edges carefully.

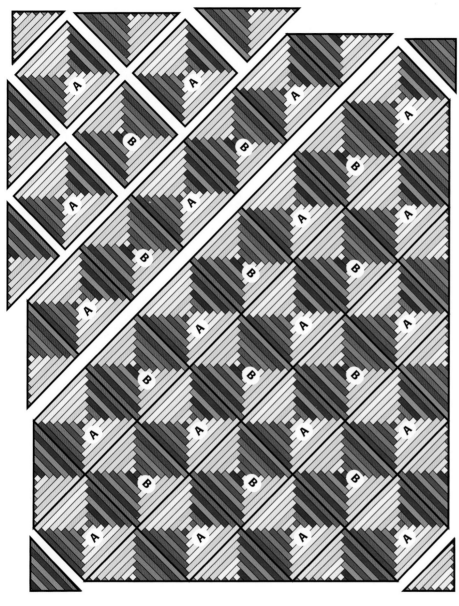

Assembly Diagram

Quilt Top Assembly

Note: Refer to **Assembly Diagram** for following steps.

3 Watching placement and orientation carefully, arrange and sew 8 diagonal rows, using setting triangles and blocks. Sew rows together. Stitch quarter-block triangles to corners. If necessary, **trim** edges even. Stitch a scant ¼″ from all edges to stabilize bias, if desired.

Quilting and Finishing

4 Layer, baste, and quilt. Maggi quilted feathered motifs in the light areas using tan thread (see **photos**). Each dark area is quilted in a continuous Greek key design in brown thread. Bind with brown texture.

Freshly Frayed

For a quick and easy quilt, raw-edge patches are appliquéd and quilted in one step. Or, send the prepared quilt top to your favorite longarm quilter for an even faster finish!

Designed by
BONNIE BAILEY
& BRENDA BAILEY

Made by
BONNIE BAILEY

Finished Quilt Size
72½" x 79½"

Note: Template, printed without seam allowance, is on page 37.

Fabric Requirements

18 assorted green, orange, pink, yellow, and brown prints (appliqué)	1 fat quarter **each***
Cream solid (background)	3⅞ yds.**
Brown/multicolor floral (appliqué, border)	1⅝ yds.
Green print (appliqué, binding)	1¼ yds.
Backing (piece lengthwise)	5 yds.
Batting size	82" x 88"

*A fat quarter is an 18" x 20-22" cut of fabric.
**Based on at least 40" of usable width.

Other Materials
Water-soluble fabric marker
Water-soluble glue*
*Bonnie and Brenda recommend Elmer's® Washable School Glue.

Planning and Marking
Appliqué shapes are positioned and glued on a grid-marked background, then secured as raw-edge appliqué during the quilting process. Test fabric marker and glue for removability on a scrap of background fabric before beginning; both must be completely removable for Bonnie and Brenda's technique.

Cutting Instructions
(cut first, before cutting appliqué)
Note: Cutting instructions for appliqué shapes are on template on **page 37**.
Cream solid
  2 rectangles width of fabric (WOF) x 66"
Brown/multicolor floral
  *4 strips 4¾" x 76", pieced from 8 WOF strips
Green print
  9 strips 2½" x WOF (binding)
*Border strips include extra length for trimming.

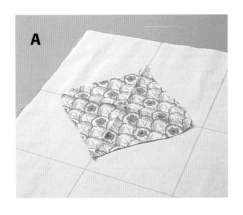

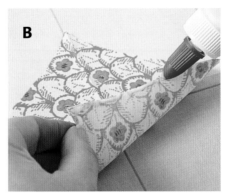

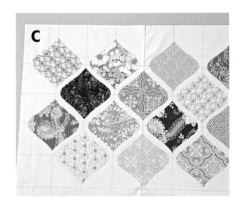

Making the Quilt Center

1 Sew 2 cream rectangles right sides together along 1 long side to make background. Open and press.

2 Finger-press background in half on both length and width. Using water-soluble fabric marker, mark lines on center creases on right side of background fabric (**Diagram I**). Beginning at creases and moving towards edges of background, mark lines 3½" apart on each side of beginning lines, until you have 17 vertical and 19 horizontal lines.

3 Finger-press Template A shape in half on both length and width. Position at intersection of 2 marked lines, centering (**photo A**).

Use a thin bead of water-soluble glue to secure all edges (**photo B**).

Repeat to add 162 total A to gridded background, staggering rows as shown (**photo C**).

4 Trim all edges of background 4" from outer marked lines (**Diagram II**).

Adding the Border

5 Referring to the **Assembly Diagram**, sew brown/multicolor floral 76" strips to sides; trim even with top and bottom. Sew remaining brown strips to top/bottom; trim even with sides.

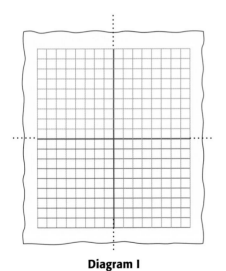

Diagram I

4¾" x 76"

4¾" x 76"

Assembly Diagram

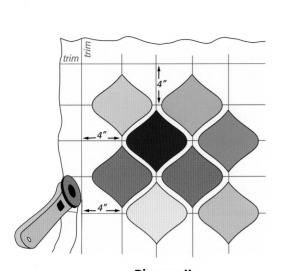

Diagram II

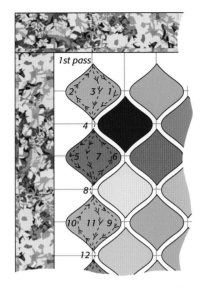

1st pass

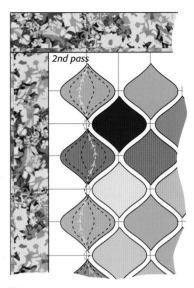

2nd pass

Diagram III

Quilting and Finishing

6 Layer, baste, and quilt. Bonnie machine quilted the appliqué a generous ¼" inside raw edges, and echo quilted a curved shape in the center of each appliqué. See **Diagram III** for suggested quilting path (notice that the 2nd quilting pass adds just 1 curved line to each already-quilted shape). The border is quilted with a continuous floral design. Bind with green print. Following manufacturer's instructions, launder quilt to remove washable marker and glue.

Freshly Frayed
Template A
Cut 144
Assorted prints
Cut 9
Brown/multicolor floral
Cut 9
Green print

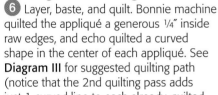

Visit
McCallsQuilting.com...for a pattern for a crib size version of this sweet quilt (click on the Bonuses tab).

The Scent of Summer

Designed by
JANELLE CEDUSKY

Machine Quilted by
SHELLY NEALON
of Quilted Bliss

Clean, colorful, contemporary prints
become rays of sunshine in this thoroughly modern throw.
If you've been looking for a way to show off lots of cool
fabrics, **here's your fast, easy pattern!**

Finished Quilt Size
48" x 62"

Note: See **page 41** for piecing template.

Fabric Requirements

Assorted large prints (piecing)	1⅝-2⅛ yds. **total**
Multicolor circles print (piecing, strips)	⅝ yd.
Lime print (piecing, binding)	1 yd.
Taupe solid (strips)	1⅛ yds.
Backing (piece widthwise)	3¼ yds.
Batting size	56" x 70"

Other Materials
See-through template plastic
Acrylic ruler, 6½" x 12" or larger

Planning and Cutting
This simple and sophisticated quilt show-cases exuberant prints that dazzle against the muted solid.

To prepare A patches, trace Template A on template plastic, including grain line. Cut out on outer marked lines. Place template on wrong side of fabric, mark around edges, and cut out fabric patch. The gentle curve is easy to sew…just follow our instructions. You may find you can accurately sew the curved seams without using any pins!

Cutting Instructions
Assorted large prints—**cut a total of:**
   27 Template A
Multicolor circles print
   *2 strips 2½" x 62", pieced from 4 width of fabric (WOF) strips
   3 Template A
Lime print
   *7 strips 2½" x WOF (binding)
   3 Template A
Taupe solid
   6 strips 3½" x 62", pieced from 10 WOF strips
*Cut first.

Piecing the Rows
1 Referring to **Diagram I**, pin bottom of 1st A patch to top of 2nd, right sides together and keeping 1st A (concave curve) on top. Align corners and pin, if desired. You may also want to pin the center. Stitch together slowly, adjusting fabric fullness as you go. Sew 11 A's together to make vertical row (**Diagram II**). Make 3 total.

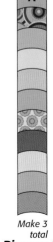

Make 3 total

Diagram I   **Diagram II**

2 Referring to **Diagram III-A**, place see-through acrylic ruler on 1st A patch of row with 4½" line on seam at highest point of curve, and perpendicular to straight edges; trim row end.

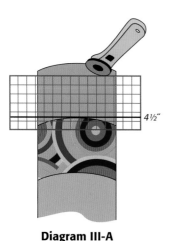

Diagram III-A

Measure 62" from freshly trimmed end and trim opposite end (**Diagram III-B**). Repeat to trim remaining rows.

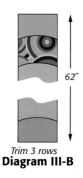

Trim 3 rows
Diagram III-B

Quilt Top Assembly
3 Referring to **Assembly Diagram** on the next page, sew together 6 taupe and 2 multicolor circles print 62" strips and trimmed rows in order and orientation shown.

Quilting and Finishing
4 Layer, baste, and quilt. Shelly machine quilted an allover pattern of spirals using variegated thread. Bind with lime print.

Bonus Queen Size

Finished Quilt Size
81" x 95½"

Fabric Requirements	
15 assorted large prints (piecing)	⅜ yd. **each**
Multicolor circles print (piecing, strips)	1⅛ yds.
Lime print (piecing, binding)	1¼ yds.
Taupe solid (strips)	2⅞ yds.
Backing (piece widthwise)	7⅝ yds.
Batting size	Queen

Cutting Instructions
15 assorted large prints—**cut from each:**
   5 Template A, cut on length-
      wise grain
Multicolor circles print
   *4 strips 2½" x 95½", pieced
      from 10 width of fabric (WOF) strips
   5 Template A, cut on length-
      wise grain
Lime print
   *10 strips 2½" x WOF
      (binding)
   5 Template A, cut on length-
      wise grain
Taupe solid
   10 strips 3½" x 95½", cut on
      lengthwise grain
*Cut first.

Piecing the Rows
5 Refer to Step 1 and **Diagram I** for piecing tips. Sew 17 A's together to make vertical row (**Diagram IV**). Make 5 total.

6 Place see-through acrylic ruler on 1st A patch of row with 4½" line on seam at highest point of curve, and perpendicular to straight edges (**Diagram III-A**); trim row end.

Measuring from freshly trimmed end, trim row to 95½" (**Diagram V**). Trim remaining rows.

Quilt Top Assembly
7 Referring to **Queen Size Assembly Diagram** on the next page, sew together 10 taupe and 4 multicolor circles print 95½" strips and 5 vertical rows in order and orientation shown.

Quilting and Finishing
8 Layer, baste, and quilt. Bind with lime print.

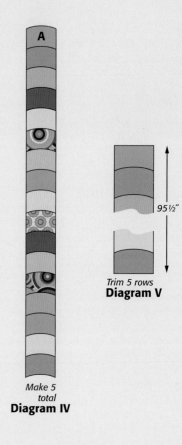

Make 5 total
Diagram IV

95½"

Trim 5 rows
Diagram V

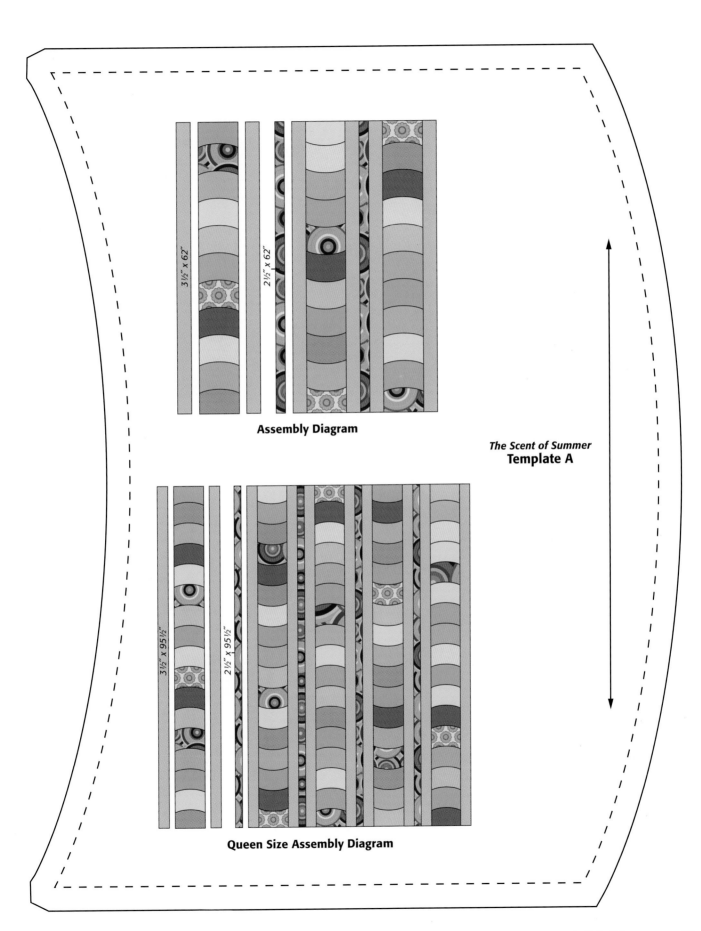

3 1/2" x 62"

2 1/2" x 62"

Assembly Diagram

The Scent of Summer
Template A

3 1/2" x 95 1/2"

2 1/2" x 95 1/2"

Queen Size Assembly Diagram

Bonjour!

The first rays of Parisian light peek through the window as the city stirs... time for fresh croissants, hot coffee, and a few more minutes lingering under this pretty quilt. **La Tour Eiffel will have to wait...**

Designed by
GERRI ROBINSON

Machine Quilted by
REBECCA SEGURA
of Zeffie's Quilts

Finished Quilt Size
88½" x 88½"

**Number of Blocks
and Finished Sizes**
4 Corner Blocks 12" x 12"
12 Edge Blocks 12" x 12"
9 Center Blocks 12" x 12"

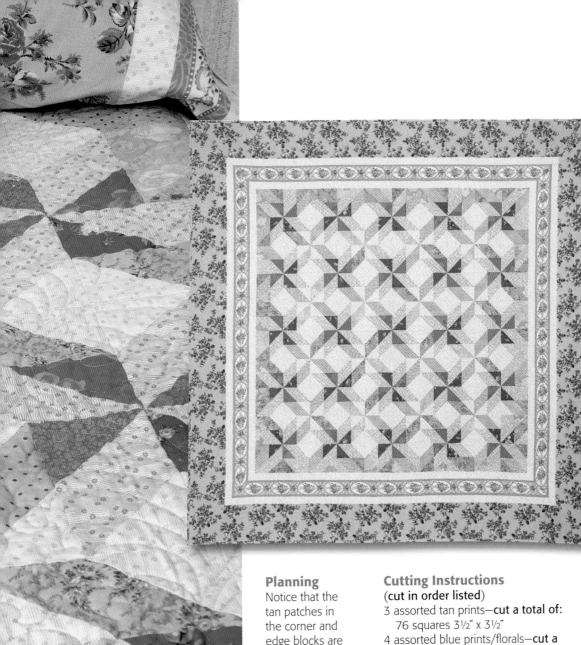

Planning

Notice that the tan patches in the corner and edge blocks are all positioned to the outside of the quilt center in this beautiful, feminine quilt.

Fabric Requirements

3 assorted tan prints (blocks)	³⁄₈ yd. **each**
4 assorted blue prints/florals (blocks)	⁵⁄₈ yd. **each**
Light pink print (blocks)	1⁷⁄₈ yds.
4 assorted dark pink prints/florals (blocks)	¹⁄₂ yd. **each**
Cream print (blocks, 1st and 3rd borders)	3¹⁄₈ yds.
Cream/pink border stripe (2nd border)	2¹⁄₂ yds.
Blue/pink floral (outer border, binding)	3⁵⁄₈ yds.
Backing	8³⁄₈ yds.
Batting size	98″ x 98″

Cutting Instructions

(cut in order listed)

3 assorted tan prints—**cut a total of:**
    76 squares 3¹⁄₂″ x 3¹⁄₂″
4 assorted blue prints/florals—**cut a total of:**
    100 rectangles 3¹⁄₂″ x 6¹⁄₂″
Light pink print
    100 rectangles 3¹⁄₂″ x 6¹⁄₂″
4 assorted dark pink prints/florals—**cut a total of:**
    100 squares 3¹⁄₂″ x 3¹⁄₂″
Cream print
    *4 strips 2″ x 80″, pieced from 8 width of fabric (WOF) strips
    *4 strips 2″ x 70″, pieced from 8 WOF strips
    224 squares 3¹⁄₂″ x 3¹⁄₂″
Cream/pink border stripe
    *4 strips 4″ x 82″, cut on lengthwise grain, centered on stripe
Blue/pink floral
    10 strips 2¹⁄₂″ x WOF (binding)
    *4 strips 8″ x 96″, cut on lengthwise grain
*Border strips include extra length for trimming.

Piecing the Blocks

1 Draw diagonal line on wrong side of assorted tan 3½″ square. Referring to **Diagram I**, place marked square on assorted blue 3½″ x 6½″ rectangle, right sides together, aligning raw edges. Sew on marked line; trim away and discard excess fabric. Open and press. Repeat on opposite end of rectangle to make pieced rectangle. Make 20 total. Make remaining pieced rectangles in colors and quantities shown.

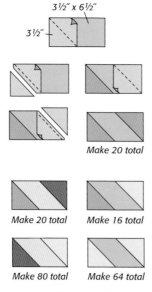

3½″ x 6½″

3½″

Make 20 total

Make 20 total   *Make 16 total*

Make 80 total   *Make 64 total*

Diagram I

2 Referring to **Diagram II-A**, sew together 8 pieced rectangles in color arrangement shown to make Corner Block. Make 4 total.

Make 4 total

Diagram II-A

In similar manner make 12 total Edge Blocks (**Diagram II-B**) and 9 total Center Blocks (**Diagram II-C**).

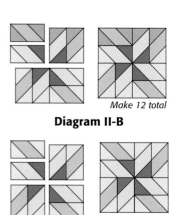

Make 12 total

Diagram II-B

Make 9 total

Diagram II-C

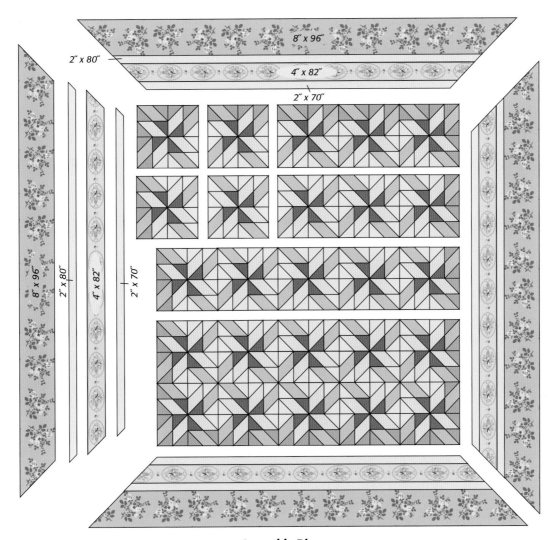

8″ x 96″

2″ x 80″

4″ x 82″

2″ x 70″

8″ x 96″ 2″ x 80″ 4″ x 82″ 2″ x 70″

Assembly Diagram

Assembling the Quilt Top

Note: Refer to **Assembly Diagram** for following steps, watching orientation.

3 Sew 2 top/bottom rows, each using 2 Corner Blocks and 3 Edge Blocks. Sew 3 center rows, each using 2 Edge Blocks and 3 Center Blocks. Stitch rows together.

4 Finger-press all border strips in half, centering on motif if desired. To make pieced border strip, stitch together cream print 70″ strip, cream/pink border stripe 82″ strip, cream 80″ strip, and blue/pink floral 96″ strip, matching folds. Make 4. Centering folds, add pieced border strips to all 4 sides of quilt (see **Add Mitered Borders** at right). Sew and trim miters.

Quilting and Finishing

5 Layer, baste, and quilt. Rebecca machine quilted an allover plume and flower design. Bind with blue/pink floral.

Add Mitered Borders

Center and pin border strips to sides, top, and bottom of quilt. Strips will extend beyond quilt top. Starting and stopping ¼″ from quilt corners and backstitching to secure, sew strips to quilt top. Press seam allowances toward quilt center. Fold quilt on diagonal, right sides together. Align border strip raw edges and border seams at the ¼″ backstitched point; pin together. Align ruler edge with fold, extending ruler completely across border. Draw line from the backstitched point to the border raw edges. Stitch on drawn line, backstitching at both ends. Press seam open. With quilt right side up, align 45°-angle line of square ruler on seam line to check accuracy. If corner is flat and square, trim excess fabric to ¼″ seam allowance. Repeat for all corners.

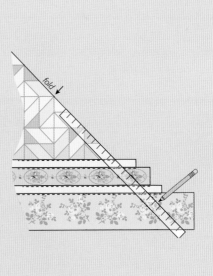

fold

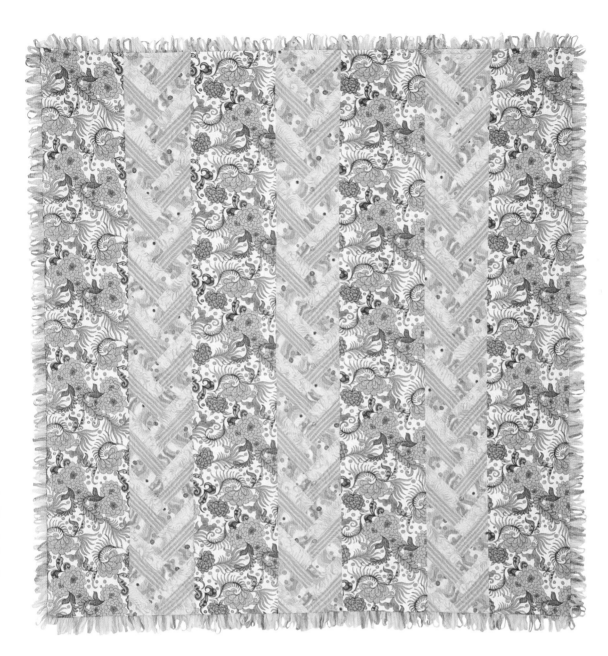

Designed by
DEBORAH A. HOBBS

Finished Quilt Size
57″ x 60″
(plus ribbon trim)

Aqua Frost

If you are looking for a fresh and different idea for finishing the edge of your quilt, look no further. Try Deborah Hobbs' looped-ribbon trim technique…our photos show you how!

Fabric Requirements*

Blue/multicolor dot **and** aqua stripe (piecing)	¾ yd. **each**
Aqua print (piecing)	⅞ yd.
White/blue/purple large floral (strips)	1⅞ yds.
Backing	4 yds.**
Batting size	66″ x 68″

*See **Planning**.
**Backing yardage and cutting instructions are based on 40-42″ wide fabric.

Other Materials

Coordinating ribbon or ribbon yarn, ⅜″-wide	60 yds.
Green **and** blue glass buttons (½″), 15 **each**	

Making the Pieced Strips

1 Referring to **Diagram I**, stitch blue 6½″ strip to short side of aqua print half-square triangle, aligning end of strip with corner of triangle. Stitch aqua stripe strip to adjacent side. In same manner, add aqua print, blue, aqua stripe, and aqua print strips, in that order. Repeat process until a total of 60 strips have been added to complete pieced strip. Make 3. You will have 1 aqua print half-square triangle left over.

2 Referring to **Diagram II**, trim ends of 6½″ strips on left side of pieced strip in a straight line perpendicular to raw edge of aqua triangle. **Trim** right side of pieced strip 7½″ from trimmed left side. **Trim** blue and striped strips at top of pieced strip even with raw edge of aqua triangle. **Trim** bottom of pieced strip to 60½″ length. Repeat process to trim remaining 2 pieced strips.

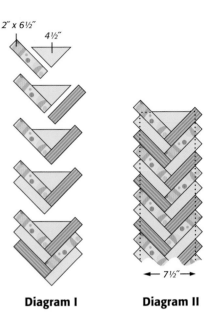

Diagram I   **Diagram II**

Planning

The luxurious touch of looped-ribbon trim was applied after quilting, using facing strips cut from the backing fabric to finish the quilt edge. Our step-by-step photos on the next page show you how.

If you prefer to finish the quilt using traditional binding, you will need an additional ¾ yd. of fabric from which to cut 7 strips 2½″ x width of fabric. Reduce backing fabric yardage to 3¾ yds. (piece widthwise).

Cutting Instructions

▱ = cut in half diagonally
Blue/multicolor dot
    60 strips 2″ x 6½″
Aqua stripe
    60 strips 2″ x 6½″, cut on
        lengthwise grain
Aqua print
    2 squares 4½″ x 4½″ ▱
    60 strips 2″ x 6½″
White/blue/purple large floral
    4 strips 9½″ x 60½″, cut on
        lengthwise grain
Backing
    2 rectangles, width of fabric
        (WOF) x 65″
    4 strips 1¼″ x 64″, pieced from
        7 WOF strips

Assembly Diagram

Quilt Top Assembly and Quilting

3 Referring to the **Assembly Diagram**, stitch 4 large floral strips and 3 trimmed pieced strips together, alternating.

4 To make backing, stitch 2 WOF x 65" rectangles together along 1 long side. Layer with batting and quilt top; baste and quilt. Deborah machine quilted an overall design of feathers and flowers. **Trim** backing and batting even with quilt top.

Finishing

5 Beginning at least 8" from any corner, align end of ribbon with raw edge of right side of trimmed quilt (**photo A**). Fold a 2" loop of ribbon and position on quilt as shown in **photo B**. Pin in place. Continue to fold 2" loops and position them next to each other all around quilt edge, pivoting at corners (**photo C**). Trim end of ribbon even with quilt. Machine stitch a scant ¼" from quilt edge, catching ends of ribbon loops in stitching, and pivoting a scant ¼" from each corner (**photos D** and **E**).

6 Press ¼" to wrong side of 1 long edge of each 1¼" x 64" facing strip. On front of quilt, place pressed strip on 1 edge, right sides together and aligning long raw edges. Backstitching ½" at beginning and end of seam, sew ¼" from long raw edge (**photo F**). Trim strip ends even with quilt. Repeat to add strips to all 4 sides of quilt. Trim corners (**photo G**). Turn facing to back of quilt. Using thread that matches quilt front, machine stitch pressed edges of facing in place (**photo H**).

7 Tack 10 buttons to center of each pieced strip on quilt front, spacing evenly and alternating colors.

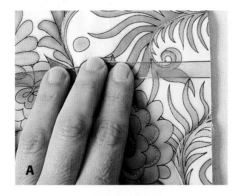

A

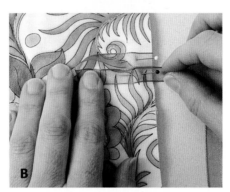

B

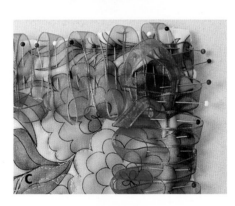

C

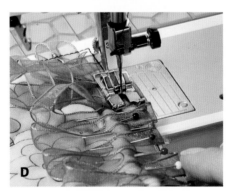

D

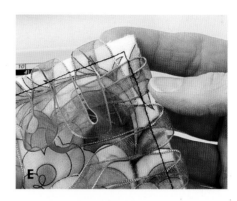

E

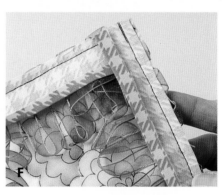

F

G

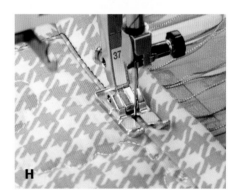

H

Li'l Skipper

Designed by
JULIE HIGGINS

Finished Quilt Size
53½" x 53½"

**Number of Blocks
and Finished Size**
13 Sailboat Blocks 8" x 8"
12 Pinwheel Blocks 8" x 8"

**Set sail for some
nautically-inspired
piecing fun** with this scrappy
throw. Stash fabrics coupled with
any cloudy sky print guarantee you
a one-of-a-kind version of this
seaworthy design.

Fabric Requirements

Assorted yellow prints/
  mottles (sails, pin-
  wheels)
	⅝-⅞ yd.
	total

Assorted blue dots/
  prints/mottles/stripes
  (blocks)
	1½-1¾
	yds.
	total

Assorted turquoise
  prints/dots/stripes
  (blocks)
	⅝-⅞ yd.
	total

Assorted red plaids/ prints (boats)	⅜-½ yd. **total**
Red/navy stripe (inner border)	½ yd.
Blue/aqua sky print (outer border)	1 yd.
Red/white dot (binding)	⅝ yd.
Backing	3⅝ yds.
Batting size	62" x 62"

Explore!

Fresh and sweet, this child's quilt is a great way to use some of your scraps. Look closely at the photos, and you'll notice that Julie had a lot of fun choosing fabrics for her sailboats. The Pinwheel breeze blows some sails to the left and some to the right. Most sailboats have sails of 2 colors aligned vertically or horizontally, but 4 have 4 matching sails. The color of the sea changes from blue to turquoise and even purple. And, while most of the Pinwheel Blocks have 2 blue fabrics, some have only 1 blue with 2 turquoise fabrics. One block even has a cream stripe!

Julie also cut some block patches from the border fabrics. If you wish to do likewise, cut border strips first and then cut patches. Experiment with your fabrics and have fun making your blocks just the way you want them. For an extra-soft quilt, you might consider using flannel fabrics.

Cutting Instructions

⊠ = cut in half twice diagonally

Assorted yellow prints/mottles—**cut a total of:**
- 26 squares 2⅞" x 2⅞"
- 12 squares 5¼" x 5¼" ⊠

Assorted blue dots/prints/mottles/stripes
- **cut 13 matching sets of:**
  - 3 squares 2⅞" x 2⅞"
  - 2 rectangles 2½" x 4½"
- **cut a total of:**
  - 8 strips 2½" x 8½"
  - 23 squares 5¼" x 5¼" ⊠

Assorted turquoise prints/dots/stripes—**cut a total of:**
- 5 strips 2½" x 8½"
- 13 squares 5¼" x 5¼" ⊠

Assorted red plaids/prints—**cut 13 matching sets of:**
- 1 square 2⅞" x 2⅞"
- 1 rectangle 2½" x 4½"

Red/navy stripe
- 4 strips 2½" x 48", pieced from 5 width of fabric (WOF) strips

Blue/aqua sky print
- 4 strips 5" x 58", pieced from 6 WOF strips

Red/white dot
- 6 strips 2½" x WOF (binding)

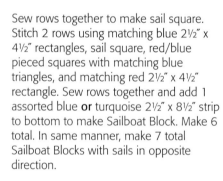

Piecing the Blocks

1 Draw diagonal line on wrong side of assorted yellow 2⅞" square. Place marked square on assorted blue 2⅞" square, right sides together (**Diagram I**). Sew ¼" seam on each side of marked line; cut apart on marked line. Press open to make pieced squares. Make 26 sets of 2 matching. In same manner, make remaining pieced squares using assorted red 2⅞" squares and remaining blue 2⅞" squares. Make 13 sets of 2 matching.

2 Watching orientation of yellow triangles and referring to **Diagram II** and photos, sew 2 rows of 2 yellow pieced squares with matching blue triangles each.

Sew rows together to make sail square. Stitch 2 rows using matching blue 2½" x 4½" rectangles, sail square, red/blue pieced squares with matching blue triangles, and matching red 2½" x 4½" rectangle. Sew rows together and add 1 assorted blue **or** turquoise 2½" x 8½" strip to bottom to make Sailboat Block. Make 6 total. In same manner, make 7 total Sailboat Blocks with sails in opposite direction.

3 Referring to **Diagram III**, sew together 1 turquoise, 2 blue, and 1 yellow 5¼" quarter-square triangles to make pieced square. Make 12 sets of 4 matching. Watching orientation, stitch together 4 matching pieced squares to make Pinwheel Block (**Diagram IV**). Make 12 total.

2⅞"

Make 26 sets of 2 matching

Make 13 sets of 2 matching

Diagram I

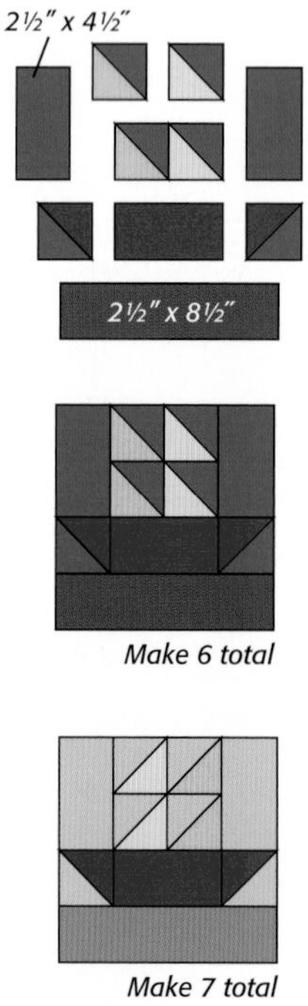

2½" x 4½"

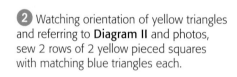

2½" x 8½"

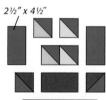

Make 6 total

Make 7 total

Diagram II

5¼"

Make 12 sets of 4 matching

Diagram III

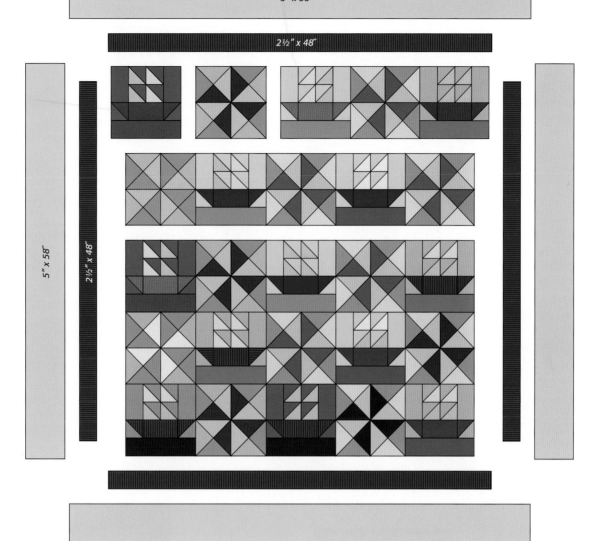

Assembly Diagram

Make 12 total

Diagram IV

Quilt Top Assembly

Note: Refer to **Assembly Diagram** and photos for following steps.

4 Watching orientation of sails, sew 3 rows using 3 Sailboat Blocks and 2 Pinwheel Blocks each, alternating. Stitch 2 rows using 3 Pinwheel Blocks and 2 Sailboat Blocks each, alternating. Sew rows together, alternating.

5 Stitch 2 red/navy strips to sides; trim even with top and bottom. Sew red/navy strips to top/bottom; trim even with sides. Sew 2 blue/aqua sky print strips to sides; trim even. Stitch sky print strips to top/bottom; trim even.

Quilting and Finishing

6 Layer, baste, and quilt. Julie machine quilted horizontal wavy lines in the sky areas of the Sailboat Blocks and vertical wavy lines in the sea strips. The Pinwheel Blocks feature angled wavy lines in all turquoise and yellow patches. A looping meander fills the outer border. Bind with red/white dot.

Photographed at Scandinavian Designs, 9000 E. Hampden, Denver, CO 80231; www.ScandinavianDesigns.com.

This richly complex look is so easy to achieve!

A beautifully striped Elementals Artisan Batik by Lunn Studios for Robert Kaufman does all the design work for you in this simply artistic throw.

Designed by
DEBRA LUNN AND
MICHAEL MROWKA

Finished Throw Size
46½" x 54½"

Fabric Requirements

Indigo/green/brown/gold batik stripe (strips)	4⅝ yds.*
Muslin (foundation)	3 yds.**
Indigo batik stripe (binding)	⅝ yd.
Backing	3¼ yds.

Rayon thread, brown (optional)
*Yardage based on featured fabric.
**Yardage based on 40" of usable width.

Planning

Can you believe this intriguing throw is made from just 1 fabric? Strips are cut diagonally from a striped batik, and sewn together on a muslin foundation to stabilize bias edges. Layer with a backing, add decorative stitching, and bind, and you've created an easy, artistic accent for your home. If you wish to add batting during the layering process, you will need a 54" x 62" piece.

Batik Illusion

Beautiful Batiks

Debra Lunn and Michael Mrowka wear the two hats of quiltmakers and fabric designers when they create Artisan Batiks for Robert Kaufman Fabrics. Their goal is to produce fabrics that will give maximum graphic and artistic impact to any project. They want to empower busy quilters to achieve beautiful results with a minimum of effort and time, and to stimulate the creative impulses of the quiltmaker who selects Artisan Batiks. Combining Debra's color expertise, Michael's three decades of graphic design experience, and the fine craftsmanship of Javanese batik makers, their fabric designs can be used to make quilts that look complex and intricate without the involved cutting and piecing usually required.

The magic of their 1″ striped batiks (used in the throw shown in this feature) is due to the well-planned, intersecting gradations of color. The stripes make easy bargello-look quilts possible. From start to finish, the throw shown above took less than a day to make.

L to R: Craftsmen carefully fold greige goods and apply dye to obtain the desired effect in these unique, gorgeously striped fabrics. Photographs courtesy of Michael Mrowka.

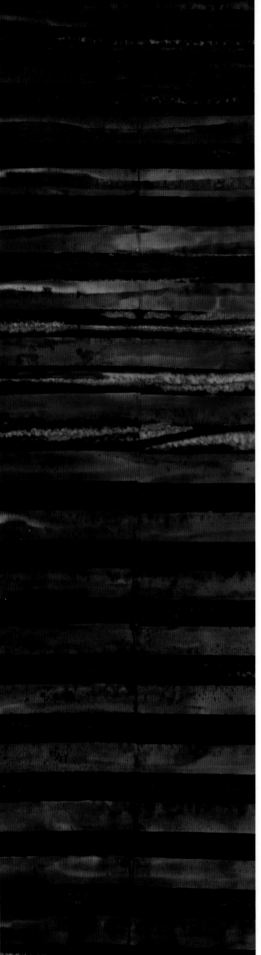

Cutting Instructions
Indigo/green/brown/gold batik stripe
  *18 bias-cut strips 3½" x 48-62"
Muslin
  1 rectangle 50" x 60", pieced from
    2 rectangles 50" x width of fabric
    (WOF)
*See **Cutting Diagram**, below.

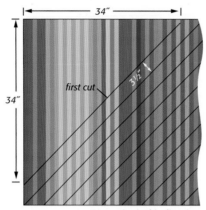

Cut 9 strips in this direction,
and 9 strips on opposite diagonal
Cutting Diagram

Assembling the Top
❶ Referring to **Diagram I**, press muslin 50" x 60" rectangle foundation in half; use fold as placement guide. Layer 2 stripe strips right sides together, 1 cut in each direction, on foundation, just touching top edge of muslin and keeping raw edges aligned with fold. Sew ¼" seam through all layers along 1 long side.

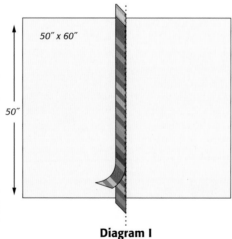

Diagram I

Press open, handling bias edges carefully (**Diagram II**). In similar manner, add strips to remaining long sides of first 2 strips, alternating direction of stripe (**Diagram III**). Continue adding strips from center out until a total of 18 strips are stitched to foundation.

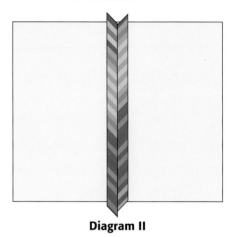

Diagram II

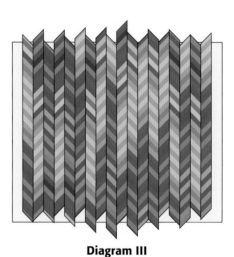

Diagram III

Finishing
❷ From backing fabric cut 2 rectangles 56" x WOF. Sew right sides together along 1 long side. Layer backing, wrong side up, and top, right side up, centering. Baste to secure. Using machine zigzag stitch (**Diagram IV**) and brown thread, stitch on each seam line, centering. **Trim** sides even with long edges of side strips. **Trim** top and bottom in straight lines perpendicular to sides. Bind with indigo batik stripe. The featured throw has blue zigzag topstitching on binding.

Diagram IV

A Gift for Mom

She'll love this snuggly shawl, complete with pretty patchwork stars and convenient pockets. It's such a fast project, you may want to make one for yourself as well!

Designed by
KARI CARR

Finished Shawl Size
22" x 72"

**Number of Blocks
and Finished Sizes**
3 Star Blocks 15" x 15"
2 Pocket Blocks 10" x 15"

Fabric Requirements	
Pink batik (blocks)	½ yd.
Dark green batik (blocks)	1 fat quarter*
Pink dot (blocks)	⅜ yd.
Light green batik **and** medium green batik (blocks)	⅝ yd. **each**
Green/pink floral (blocks, border, binding)	1⅝ yds.
White/pink dot (pocket linings)	½ yd.
Backing	1⅞ yds.
Batting size	42" x 80"
Hook and loop fastener	¾" x 2½" piece

*A fat quarter is an 18" x 20-22" cut of fabric.

Planning
Kari's cozy shawl design is perfect for Mom or for you! Lined pockets keep tissues, the remote control, or small quilting supplies handy. The featured shawl was backed with fleece fabric for extra softness.

Traditionalists will love this country-colors version.

Cutting Instructions

(cut in order listed)

▱ = cut in half diagonally

⊠ = cut in half twice diagonally

Pink batik
  12 squares 3⅜" x 3⅜"
  36 squares 3" x 3"
Dark green batik
  16 squares 3⅜" x 3⅜"
Pink dot
  5 squares 5½" x 5½"
  4 squares 3⅜" x 3⅜"
  8 squares 3" x 3"
Light green batik
  4 squares 3⅜" x 3⅜" ▱
  52 squares 3" x 3"
Medium green batik
  1 square 6¼" x 6¼" ⊠
  16 squares 5½" x 5½"
Green/pink floral
  *2 strips 3¾" x 76", pieced
    from 4 WOF strips
  **6 strips 2½" x width of
    fabric (WOF) **or** 1 square
    24" x 24" (binding)
  2 rectangles 13¾" x 15½"
  20 squares 3" x 3"
White/pink dot
  2 rectangles 11" x 16"
Backing
  2 rectangles 30" x WOF
Batting
  1 strip 30" x 80"
  2 rectangles 11" x 16"

*Border strips include extra length for trimming.

Cut WOF strips for straight-grain binding. If planning **curved corners for shawl, cut square for 2½"-wide bias-cut binding (see **Basic Quiltmaking Instructions** for **How to Make Continuous Bias**).

Piecing the Blocks

1 Draw diagonal line on wrong side of pink batik 3⅜" square. Place marked square on dark green batik 3⅜" square, right sides together (**Diagram I-A**). Sew ¼" seam on each side of marked line; cut apart on marked line. Open and press to make 2 pieced squares. Make 24.

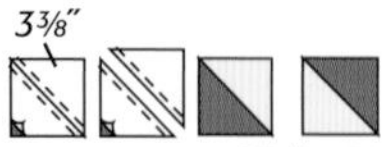

Make 24

Diagram I-A

In same manner, use dark green batik and pink dot squares to make 8 pieced squares (**Diagram I-B**).

Make 8

Diagram I-B

2 Referring to **Diagram II-A**, sew together 1 each pink batik and light green batik 3" squares and 2 pink batik/dark green pieced squares to make corner square. Make 4.

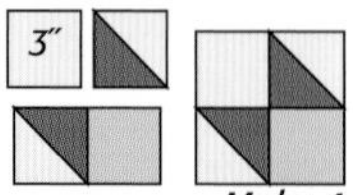

Make 4

Diagram II-A

In same manner, make remaining corner squares in fabric combinations and quantities shown in **Diagrams II-B** and **C**.

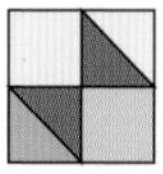

Make 4

Diagram II-B

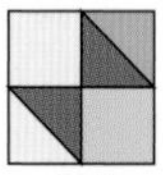

Make 4

Diagram II-C

3 Draw diagonal line on wrong side of pink batik 3" square. Place marked square on medium green batik 5½" square, right sides together, aligning raw edges (**Diagram III-A**). Sew on marked line; trim away and discard excess fabric. Open and press. Repeat process, adding 3" squares to remaining corners in fabrics shown, to make edge square. Make 12.

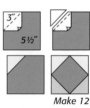

Make 12

Diagram III-A

In same manner, make center squares and remaining edge squares in fabric combinations and quantities shown in **Diagrams III-B** and **C**.

Make 5

Make 4

Diagram III-B   Diagram III-C

4 Sew 2 light green 3⅜" half-square triangles to medium green 6¼" quarter-square triangle to make pieced rectangle (**Diagram IV**). Make 4.

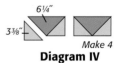

Make 4

Diagram IV

5 Referring to **Diagram V-A**, sew 3 rows using 4 corner squares, 4 edge squares, and 1 center square. Sew rows together to make Star Block. Make 2. In same manner, make remaining Star Block in arrangement shown in **Diagram V-B**.

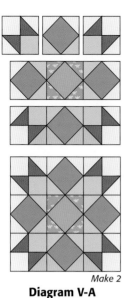

Make 2

Diagram V-A

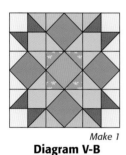

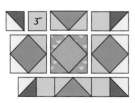

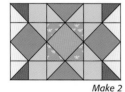

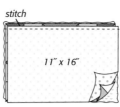

11″ x 16″

Diagram VII-A

8 Turn right side out (**Diagram VII-B**). Baste ¼″ from raw edges of block. Topstitch ¼″ from finished edge. Lightly quilt to hold layers together. The featured shawl's pockets are machine quilted in the ditch. **Trim** lining and batting even with block raw edges if needed.

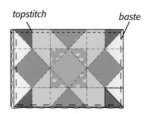

topstitch   baste

Diagram VII-B

9 Place quilted pocket on green/pink floral rectangle, right sides up, aligning sides and bottom (**Diagram VII-C**). Baste sides and bottom through all layers. Repeat Steps 7-9 to make 2nd pocket unit.

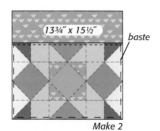

13¾″ x 15½″   baste

Make 2

Diagram VII-C

Assembling the Shawl

10 Referring to the **Assembly Diagram** and watching placement and orientation, sew together pocket units and Star Blocks. Stitch green/pink floral 76″ strips to long sides; trim even with short sides.

Make 1

Diagram V-B

6 To make Pocket Block, sew 3 rows as shown in **Diagram VI**. Sew rows together. Make 2.

3″

Make 2

Diagram VI

Making the Pocket Units

7 Referring to **Diagram VII-A**, layer batting rectangle, Pocket Block (right side up), and white/pink dot rectangle (right side down), aligning and centering along 1 long edge. Sew ¼″ from aligned raw edge, through all layers. Trim away batting in seam allowance close to stitching.

Quilting and Finishing

11 Sew backing 30″ x WOF rectangles together along 1 short side. Layer, baste, and quilt, avoiding pockets. In the featured shawl, Star Blocks are machine quilted with large motifs, and floral border areas are filled with a continuous swirl design.

12 Cut hook and loop fastener into 2 segments 1¼″ each. Hand stitch inside pockets to create secure closures. Bind shawl with green/pink floral*.

*Optional curved finish: After quilting, trim backing and batting even with shawl top. Use a small plate to trace curves on shawl corners. **Trim** even with traced lines. Bind with bias-cut green/pink floral.

Visit

McCallsQuilting.com...
for more star block patterns. Click on Blocks & Patterns, and then Quilt Block Reference.

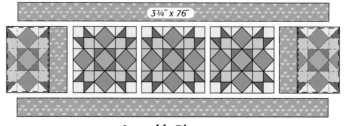

3¾″ x 76″

Assembly Diagram

Designed by
JOHN KUBINIEC

**Finished Wall
Hanging Size**
31½″ x 37½″

**Number of Blocks
and Finished Size**
12 Churn Dash
Blocks 5″ x 5″

Vibrant colors pop against a black background in this striking quilt. With a project this quick, you can add a touch of Amish quilting tradition to your home, even if you're a time-challenged modern quilter!

Amish Glow

Fabric Requirements

Assorted purple and blue solids (blocks)	3/8-7/8 yd. **total**
Black solid (blocks, border, binding)	1 3/8 yds.
Gray solid (blocks, sashing)	1/2 yd.
Fuchsia solid (sashing posts)	1/8 yd.
Backing	1 3/8 yds.
Batting size	38" x 44"

Planning
John used black and gray patches interchangeably in his block piecing, and placed assorted purple and blue patches randomly, giving this striking little quilt depth and additional interest. The wide black border is a perfect place to showcase machine or hand quilting.

Cutting Instructions
(cut in order listed)
Assorted purple and blue solids—**cut a total of:**
   24 squares 2 7/8" x 2 7/8"
   48 squares 1 1/2" x 1 1/2"
Black solid
   4 strips 2 1/2" x width of fabric (binding)
   *4 strips 6 1/2" x 36"
   17 squares 2 7/8" x 2 7/8"
   48 squares 1 1/2" x 1 1/2"
Gray solid
   7 squares 2 7/8" x 2 7/8"
   31 strips 1 1/2" x 5 1/2"
   12 squares 1 1/2" x 1 1/2"
Fuchsia solid
   20 squares 1 1/2" x 1 1/2"
*Border strips include extra length for trimming.

Piecing the Blocks
① Draw diagonal line on wrong side of assorted purple or blue 2 7/8" square. Place marked square on black or gray 2 7/8" square, right sides together (**Diagram I**). Sew 1/4" seam on each side of marked line; cut apart on marked line. Open and press to make 2 pieced squares. Make 48 total.

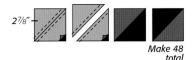

2 7/8"

Make 48 total

Diagram I

② Sew together 1 black or gray and 1 purple or blue 1 1/2" square to make pieced rectangle (**Diagram II**). Make 48 total.

1 1/2"

Make 48 total

Diagram II

③ Referring to **Diagram III**, sew 3 rows using 4 pieced squares, 4 pieced rectangles, and 1 black or gray 1 1/2" square. Sew rows together to make Churn Dash Block. Make 12 total.

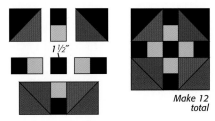

1 1/2"

Make 12 total

Diagram III

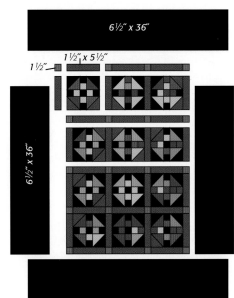

6 1/2" x 36"

1 1/2" x 5 1/2"

1 1/2"

6 1/2" x 36"

Assembly Diagram

Assembling the Quilt Top
Note: Refer to **Assembly Diagram** for following steps.

④ Sew 5 sashing rows of 4 fuchsia squares and 3 gray 5 1/2" strips each. Sew 4 block rows of 4 gray strips and 3 blocks each. Sew rows together, alternating.

⑤ Stitch black 36" strips to sides; trim even with top and bottom. Stitch remaining 36" strips to top/bottom; trim even with sides.

Quilting and Finishing
⑥ Layer, baste, and quilt. John machine quilted 2 concentric circles on each block. Sashing is stitched in the ditch. A diagonal grid fills the border. Bind with black solid.

Visit
McCallsQuilting.com...for a pattern for a lap size (62 1/2" x 74 1/2") version of this quilt. Click on Bonuses, and then McCall's Bonuses.

Basic Quiltmaking Instructions

All fabric requirements are based on 40"/42"-wide fabric.

The yardage given includes an additional 5% to account for fabric shrinkage and individual differences in cutting.

A ¼" seam allowance is included on pattern pieces when required.

All measurements for pieces, sashing, and borders include ¼" seam allowances.

The finished quilt size is the size of the quilt before quilting.

Because each quiltmaker usually has a personal preference, the type of batting to be used for each quilt will not be listed, unless it is necessary to obtain a specific look.

These instructions offer a brief introduction to quiltmaking. Quiltmaking instructions for projects in this issue are written for the individual with some sewing experience. Review this information if you are making your first quilt.

SUPPLIES
Scissors (for paper and template plastic)
Iron and ironing board
Marking tools: pencils, chalk markers, fine-point permanent marker (such as Pilot or Sharpie®)
Needles: package of sharps (for hand piecing) assorted sizes; package of betweens (for hand quilting), size Nos. 8 to 12
Quilting hoop or frame
Pins and pincushion
Rotary cutter and mat (at least 18" x 24")

Rulers: 2" x 18"; clear acrylic 12" square; clear acrylic 6" x 24" (for use with a rotary cutter)
Sewing machine (for machine piecing)
Shears, 8" (for fabric)
Template plastic
Thimble to fit the middle finger of your sewing hand
Thread: cotton thread or monofilament, size .004 (for machine quilting); quilting thread (for hand quilting); sewing thread in colors to match your fabrics

FABRIC PREPARATION
Pre-wash fabric to remove excess dye and minimize shrinking of completed project. Machine wash gently in warm water, dry on warm setting, and press. Immerse a swatch of fabric in a clear glass of water to test colorfastness; if dye appears, soak fabric in equal parts of white vinegar and water. Rinse and dry fabric; test another swatch. If dye still appears, do not use the fabric.

PRESSING
Proper pressing is a prerequisite for accurate piecing. Press with a light touch, using iron tip and an up and down movement. Save continuous motion "ironing" for wrinkled fabric. Use either steam or dry heat, whichever works best, and assembly-type pressing to save time.

Choose a pressing plan before beginning a project and stay consistent, if possible. Seams are "set" by first being pressed flat and then pressed either to one side, usually toward the darker fabric, or open. Sometimes, both are used in the same project, depending on the design.

To prevent distortion, press long, sewn strips widthwise and avoid raw bias edges. Other pressing hints are: use distilled water, avoid a too-hot iron which will cause fabric

shininess, and pre-treat wrinkled or limp fabric with a liberal amount of spray fabric sizing.

TEMPLATES
Make templates by placing transparent plastic over the printed template pattern and tracing with a fine-point permanent marker. Trace and cut out on the stitching line (broken line) for hand-piecing templates; cut on the outer solid line for machine-piecing templates.

Label each template with the name of the quilt, template letter, grain line, and match points (dots) where sewing lines intersect. Pierce a small hole at each match point for marking match points on fabric.

FABRIC MARKING & CUTTING
Position fabric wrong side up, and place the template on the fabric. With a marker or well-sharpened pencil, trace around the template and mark match points. For hand-piecing templates, allow enough space for ¼" seam allowances to be added. For machine-piecing templates, cut along the drawn line. For hand-piecing, cut ¼" beyond the drawn line.

PIECING
Stitch fabric pieces together for patchwork by hand or machine.

Hand Piecing
Place two fabric pieces right sides together. With point of pin, match corner or other match points to align seamlines; pin. Use about an 18"-long single strand of quality sewing thread and sewing needle of your choice. To secure thread, begin at a match point and, without a knot, take a stitch and a backstitch on the seamline. Make smooth running stitches, closely and evenly spaced, stitching on the drawn line on both patches of fabric. Backstitch at the end of the seam-

How to Make Continuous Bias

① Measure the quilt to determine how many inches of binding you need. Allow 10" extra for turning corners and the closure. Refer to chart to find the size square needed.

② Cut the square in half diagonally (see **Diagrams A-C**). With right sides together, sew the triangles together with a ¼" seam and press open.

③ On fabric wrong side long edges, draw lines to make strips of your chosen binding width (see **Diagram D**). Use a clear acrylic rotary ruler and a pencil or fine-point permanent pen to draw the lines.

④ Bring the short diagonal edges together (see **Diagrams E** and **F**), forming a tube. Offset the drawn lines by one strip. With right sides together, match lines with pins at the ¼" seamline and stitch seam; press open.

⑤ With scissors, cut along continuously drawn line (see **Diagram G**).

line. Do not stitch into the seam allowances. Press seams after the block is completed.

To join seamed pieces and strengthen the intersection, stitch through the seam allowances, and backstitch directly before and immediately after them.

Machine Piecing

Use a ¼"-wide presser foot for a seaming guide, or place a strip of opaque tape on the machine throat plate ¼" from the needle position. Place 2 fabric pieces right sides together, raw edges aligned, and pin perpendicular to the future seamline to secure. Begin and end stitching at the raw edges without backstitching; do not sew over pins. Make sure the thread tension and stitches are smooth and even on both sides of the seam. When joining seamed pieces, butt or match seams, pin to secure, and stitch. Press each seam before continuing to the next.

To chain-piece, repeatedly feed pairs of fabric pieces under the presser foot while taking a few stitches without any fabric under the needle between pairs. Cut the chained pieces apart before or after pressing.

APPLIQUÉING
Hand Appliqué

Needle-Turn Method. Place the template on the fabric right side. Draw around the template with a non-permanent marking tool of your choice, making a line no darker than necessary to be visible. Cut out the shape, including a scant ¼" seam allowance on all sides. Experience makes "eye-balling" the seam allowance quick and easy.

To blind stitch the appliqué shapes, position the appliqué shape on the background fabric, securing with a pin or a dab of glue stick. Select a sewing thread color to match the appliqué fabric. A 100% cotton thread is less visible than a cotton/polyester blend.

Begin stitching on a straight or gently curved edge, not at a sharp point or corner. Turn under a short length of seam allowance using your fingers and the point of your needle. Insert the needle into the seamline of the appliqué piece, coming

up from the wrong side and catching just one or two threads on the edge. Push the needle through the background fabric exactly opposite the point where the thread was stitched onto the appliqué fabric piece. Coming up from the wrong side, take a stitch through the background fabric and appliqué piece, again catching just a couple threads of the appliqué fabric. Allow about ⅛" between stitches. The thread is visible on the wrong side of your block and almost invisible on the right side.

As you stitch around the edge of an appliqué fabric piece, turn under the seam allowance as you work, following the drawn line on the right side of the fabric, using your fingers and the point of the needle.

Freezer Paper Method I. Trace the template shape onto the dull side of freezer paper and cut out. With a dry iron, press the freezer paper shape, shiny side down, onto the appliqué fabric right side. Cut out the fabric, including a scant ¼" seam allowance on all sides. To stitch, follow the same procedure used in the Needle-Turn Method. Rather than using the drawn line as your guide, use the edge of the freezer paper.

Freezer Paper Method II. Trace the template shape onto the dull side of freezer paper and cut out. With a dry iron, press the freezer paper shape, shiny side down, onto the appliqué fabric wrong side. Cut out the fabric, including a scant ¼" seam allowance on all sides. Finger-press the seam allowance to the back of the paper template and baste in place. To stitch an appliqué fabric piece, follow the same procedure used in the Needle-Turn Method. The seam allowance has already been turned under in this technique. To remove the freezer paper, shortly before closing the appliqué, remove the basting and pluck out the freezer paper with a tweezers; or after the appliqué is sewn, cut the background fabric away behind the appliqué and remove the paper.

To reverse appliqué, two fabric pieces are layered on the background fabric, the edges of the top fabric are cut in a particular design and turned under to reveal the underlying fabric. Pin or glue the

bottom appliqué fabric into position on the background block. Cut the top fabric along the specified cutting lines. Place the top fabric over the bottom fabric; check the position of the bottom fabric by holding the block up to a light source and pin. Use the Needle-Turn Method to turn under the top fabric seam allowance and appliqué, and to reveal the fabric underneath.

Machine Appliqué

Trace templates without seam allowances on paper side of paper-backed fusible web. Cut out, leaving a small margin beyond the drawn lines. Following manufacturer's instructions, apply to wrong side of appliqué fabric. Cut out on drawn line. Position appliqué on quilt where desired, and fuse to quilt following manufacturer's instructions. Finish appliqué edges by machine using a buttonhole stitch, satin stitch, or stitch of your choice.

MITERING CORNERS

Miter border corners when an angled seam complements the overall design of the quilt. Cut border strips the finished length and width of the quilt plus 4"-6" extra.

Center and pin border strips in place. Start and end seams ¼" from raw edges; backstitch to secure. Press seams away from quilt center. Lay quilt top right side up on ironing board and fold each border end flat back onto itself, right sides together, forming a 45° angle at the quilt's corner. Press to form sharp creases. Fold quilt on diagonal, right sides together. Align border strip raw edges, border seams at the ¼" backstitched point, and creases; pin in place. Stitch along crease, backstitching at ¼" border seam. Press seam open. With quilt right side up, align 45°-angle line of square ruler on seamline to check accuracy. If corner is flat and square, trim excess fabric to ¼" seam allowance.

For multiple mitered borders, sew strips together first and attach to quilt as one unit.

MARKING QUILTING PATTERNS

Press quilt top and change any correctable irregularities. Choose a marking

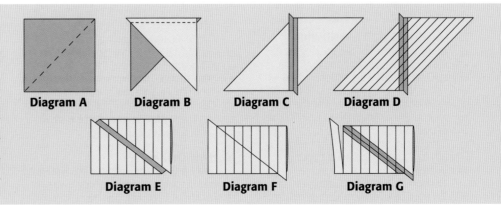

SIZE SQUARE TO CUT

Length Needed	2"-Wide Bias Strip	2½"-Wide Bias Strip	3"-Wide Bias Strip
110"	16" square	18" square	20" square
220"	23" square	26" square	28" square
340"	28" square	32" square	35" square
480"	33" square	37" square	40" square

Diagram A **Diagram B** **Diagram C** **Diagram D**

Diagram E **Diagram F** **Diagram G**

tool which makes a thin accurate line, and pre-test removability on quilt fabric scraps.

Marking tool options include: water-soluble and air-erasable markers, white dressmaker's pencil, chalk pencils, chalk rolling markers, and slivers of hardened soap. Try silver and yellow Berol® pencils on dark fabrics and a No. 2 pencil sparingly on light fabric. The same project may need several types of markers.

Design aid options include: freezer-paper cutouts, stencils, templates, household items such as cookie cutters, and acrylic rulers.

After marking quilting designs of choice, do not press quilt top; markings could be set permanently.

BACKING

Use the same quality backing fabric as used in the quilt top. Remove selvages and cut backing at least 4″ larger than quilt top on all sides. It is necessary to seam backing for quilts larger than 36″ wide when using standard 44″/45″-wide fabric. Use either vertical or horizontal seaming, whichever requires less fabric. Press backing seams open.

BATTING

Standard pre-cut batting sizes are:

Crib	45″ x 60″
Twin	72″ x 90″
Double	81″ x 96″
Queen	90″ x 108″
King	120″ x 120″

Consider several factors when choosing batting. How do you want the quilt to look? How close will the quilting stitches be? Are you hand or machine quilting? How will the quilt be used?

Batting is made from different fibers (not all fibers are available in all sizes). If you prefer an old-fashioned looking quilt, consider using a mostly cotton batting. The newer cotton battings are bonded and do not require the close quilting that old-fashioned cotton battings once did. If you don't want to do a lot of quilting, use a regular or low-loft polyester batting. If you like "puffy" quilts, use a high-loft polyester batting. Wool battings are also available.

If you are not sure which batting is right for your project, consult the professionals at your local quilt shop.

LAYERING THE QUILT SANDWICH

Mark the center of the backing on the wrong side at the top, bottom, and side edges. On a smooth, flat surface a little larger than the quilt, place backing right side down. Smooth any wrinkles until the backing is flat; use masking tape to hold it taut and in place.

Unfold batting and lay over backing. Smooth wrinkles, keeping the backing wrinkle free.

Position quilt top on backing and batting, keeping all layers wrinkle free. Match centers of quilt top with backing. Use straight pins to keep layers from shifting while basting.

BASTING

Basting holds the three layers together to prevent shifting while quilting.

For hand quilting, baste using a long needle threaded with as long a length of sewing thread as can be used without tangling. Insert needle through all layers in center of quilt and baste layers together with a long running stitch. For the first line of basting, stitch up and down the vertical center of the quilt. Next, baste across the horizontal center of the quilt. Working toward the edges and creating a grid, continue basting to completely stabilize the layers.

For machine quilting, pin-baste using nickel-plated safety pins, instead of needle and thread. Begin in the center of the quilt and work outward to the edges, placing safety pins approximately every 4″.

QUILTING
Hand Quilting

Hand quilting features evenly spaced, small stitches on both sides of the quilt with no knots showing on the back.

Most quilters favor 100% cotton thread in ecru or white, though beautiful colors are available.

Beginners start with a size 8 or 9 "between" needle and advance to a shorter, finer size 10 or 12 needle for finer stitching. Use a well-fitting, puncture-proof thimble on the middle finger of your sewing hand to position and push the needle through the quilt layers.

A frame or hoop keeps the layered quilt smooth and taut; choose from a variety of shapes and sizes. Select a comfortable seat with proper back support and a good light source, preferably natural light, to reduce eye strain.

To begin, cut thread 24″ long and make a knot on one end. Place the needle tip either into a seamline or ½″ behind the point where quilting stitches are to begin and guide it through the batting and up through the quilt top to "bury" the knot. Gently pull on the thread until you hear the knot "pop" through the quilt top. Trim the thread tail.

To quilt using a running stitch, hold the needle parallel to the quilt top and stitch up and down through the three layers with a rocking motion, making several stitches at a time. This technique is called stacking. Gently and smoothly pull the thread through the layers. To end, make a small knot and bury it in the batting.

Machine Quilting

Machine quilting requires an even-feed or walking foot to ensure quilting a straight stitch without distorting the layers, and a darning foot for free-motion or heavily curved stitching.

Use 100% cotton thread or size .004 monofilament thread (clear for light-colored fabrics, smoky for dark fabrics) on the top and cotton in the bobbin. Pre-test stitch length and thread tension using two muslin pieces layered with batting. Adjust as needed.

Choose a quilting strategy. Begin stitching in the middle and work outward, making sure the layers are taut. Roll the edges of the quilt compactly to reveal the area being quilted; reroll as needed. To secure the thread, take 1 or 2 regular-length stitches forward, backward, and continue forward; stitch a few very small stitches and gradually increase to desired length. Trim thread tails.

Stitch "in the ditch" or along the seamline to secure quilt layers while adding subtle texture. Stitch open areas with a design of your choice.

MAKING BINDING STRIPS

Quilt binding can be cut on the bias or straight of grain. Use a continuous strip of bias for a quilt that will be used frequently or has scalloped edges and rounded corners. Refer to "How To Make Continuous Bias" on pages 62 and 63 for making continuous bias binding. For bias or straight-grain double-fold binding, cut 2½″- or 3″-wide strips of fabric and fold in half, wrong sides together.

ATTACHING THE BINDING

Beginning near the middle of any side, align binding and quilt raw edges. Sew to the corner and stop stitching ¼″ from the quilt edge; backstitch to secure (an even-feed foot is very helpful). Remove from sewing machine. Fold the binding strip up and back down over itself, aligning raw edges on the second side, and pin in place. Beginning ¼″ from the quilt edge (same point where stitching stopped on the first side), sew binding to second side and stop stitching ¼″ from next corner edge; backstitch. Remove from sewing machine and continue in the same manner. After sewing all sides, finish using the technique of your choice. Wrap binding around to the back side, using your fingers to manipulate each corner to achieve a miter on both front and back sides. Pin and blindstitch in place.

SIGNING YOUR QUILT

You will want to sign and date your quilt and record other information important to you, such as the quilt's name, your city and state, and the event the quilt commemorates. You may embroider or use permanent ink to record this information on a piece of fabric that you then stitch to the quilt backing, or you may embroider directly on the quilt.